Swimming In Quicksand:

Dog-Paddling Your Way To Career Success

Scott A. Koon

Scott A. Koon

Swimming In Quicksand

Copyright © 2014 Scott A. Koon

All rights reserved.

ISBN-10: 1494918080

ISBN-13: 978-1494918088

Scott A. Koon

DEDICATION

This book is dedicated to "My Ladies". Merri and Daria make our house a home and me proud to be a husband and father.

Swimming In Quicksand

Scott A. Koon

Table of Contents

CHAPTER 1 – Another Day in Paradise 1

CHAPTER 2 – Fun At Home, Too 4

CHAPTER 3 – Hope 9

CHAPTER 4 – Introductions 13

CHAPTER 5 – Things Are Looking Up 20

CHAPTER 6 – The Overview 24

CHAPTER 7 – Homework 33

CHAPTER 8 – Objectives, Options, And Obstacles 43

CHAPTER 9 – Maribelle's Story 50

CHAPTER 10 – The Operational Plan 55

CHAPTER 11—Implementation 58

CHAPTER 12 – The Test 61

CHAPTER 13 – Fallout 66

CHAPTER 14 – Loose Ends 72

CHAPTER 15 – The Rest Of Maribelle's Story 77

CHAPTER 16 – The Surprise 81

CHAPTER 17 – One Year Later 84

CHAPTER 18 – Coaching Overview 91

Swimming In Quicksand

ACKNOWLEDGMENTS

This book wouldn't exist without Mary Ann Djonne and James Arnott who introduced me to coaching and showed me how it can change lives. Kirk Weisler has been inspirational to me since the day we met. He taught me, and reminds me daily, about the power of taking control of your own life. Last, but certainly not least, Merri and Daria have supported me and showed interest in my plans to write, and excitement as I kept moving forward.

Swimming In Quicksand

CHAPTER 1 – Another Day in Paradise

Mark checked his watch as he walked into the building.

"Dang it, 8:15 again. This is the third time I've been late this week," he said to himself under his breath. He jogged up the stairs, and hurried past several of his co-workers. In his office, he flipped on the lights, tossed his coat onto the visitor chair, and was sitting down when the phone rang.

"Great," he mumbled as he picked up the phone, "looks like it's going to be a 'wonderful' day."

"Mark Johnson, Information Technology," he said.

"Mark, this is Derek Sanders. How are you this morning?"

"Great." Mark sat up straight. "What can I help you with?" Was this about the interview? Derek had told him it would be at least a week before they made a decision. It was about time he heard. The suspense was killing him.

"Listen," said Derek, "I'm calling about last week..."

Mark thought back to last Wednesday. It had gone very well. In fact, he couldn't remember ever feeling so good about an interview. While he'd been nervous at the beginning, by the end he was feeling relaxed and all five members of the panel were smiling and nodding.

"I nailed it," he thought to himself.

"Mark, I wanted to thank you for your interest in our position, but we've decided to offer it to someone else."

Mark was stunned. "Wow," he said. "Was there something I could or should have done differently?"

"No. You interviewed very well. The whole panel agreed you made the decision very difficult. The bottom line is that you didn't have as much large project management experience as the other candidate. With the work we have lined up and the organizational changes we have planned, we believe the other candidate will be more successful."

"Okay," Mark said, "thank you so much for calling."

"Not a problem. Thank you for your interest in our position. Take care." The line went dead.

Mark slowly hung up the phone, closed his eyes, and leaned back in his chair. Just then, he heard a loud double knock at his door.

"Boss!" said a deep loud voice from the hall.

Mark took a deep breath and turned toward the door. "Yes James?"

"Where have you been? I stopped by twice and you weren't here."

"I'm here now."

"Good, because there is a crisis you need to address, now!" James lunged through the door and leaned over, putting his nose within an inch of Mark's. "I refuse to work with Frank! He's insulting and unprofessional. He has no right to criticize my work. I've worked for Oracle Corporation and consulted with Fortune 500 companies! What has he done? What education does he have that gives him the right to question my decisions? If he's so smart, he can do the upgrades by himself. You need to tell him that, because I refuse to talk to him!" And before Mark could say anything, James turned and stormed out of the office.

"Yep," he said to the empty office, "just another day in

paradise."

The rest of the day didn't go any better. He was at least ten minutes late for all of his meetings, one of which was with his supervisor. At four o'clock, he was trying to complete at least one to-do list item when John from down the hall stopped by to yell at him for not turning in the policy revisions due at 5pm yesterday.

Finally, at five he signed off his workstation, grabbed his coat and headed, angrily, for the door. "Enough is enough," he said through clenched teeth. "God, I hate this job."

CHAPTER 2 – Fun At Home, Too

The drive home only made things worse. Traffic was terrible. He knew he shouldn't have taken the expressway, but he was so frustrated about work he didn't notice his mistake until traffic came to a complete standstill.

"Dammit!" He slammed his hand against the top of the steering wheel. "How could I have been so stupid? It's going to take me forever to get home!" He felt the muscles in his neck start to tense and his blood start to boil. He leaned his head back and screamed at the top of his lungs. "Ahhhhhhhhhhh!" He looked to his left and the man in the car next to him was looking at him like he'd lost his mind. Mark could feel the blood rushing to his cheeks. He quickly looked at his lap and avoided eye contact with everyone around him.

By the time he pulled into his garage, it was 6:30. An hour and a half to go 29 miles! Absolutely ridiculous! He climbed out of his car, slammed the door and walked into the kitchen, punching the garage door button as he walked past.

Maggie looked up from the kitchen table as he stormed in. "Mark, you're late again. Is everything all right? We held dinner for twenty minutes. When you still weren't here we decided to start without you."

"Everything is just fine." He stomped past her into the office, dropped his stuff on the desk, and stomped back into the kitchen.

As he was pulling out his chair, Maggie said, "We were worried about you. We heard on the radio there was an accident on the expressway. When you didn't call we worried you might have been involved."

Mark looked at his wife and daughter. Maggie's brown eyes framed by her short brown hair were flashing concern and a hint of anger. He glanced at his daughter, Denise. While her hair was longer, she looked just like her mother, including the look in her eyes. He took a deep breath. "Sorry. I was so angry at the traffic it never occurred to me to call." He sat down at the table and started spooning casserole onto his plate.

"I guess we don't need to ask how your day went," said Maggie.

"About the same as yesterday," he replied.

Denise raised her hand. "I had a bad day, too, Daddy."

"Really? What happened?" Mark asked, relieved to talk about something besides work and traffic.

"Well, one of the other girls at school pushed me down, then she and two of her friends wouldn't let me get to my locker. I ended up being late for class." She continued talking, but Mark wasn't listening. Hearing about the girl at school reminded him of James--his big booming voice, his tendency to knock loudly, blame others, and expect others to change so he wouldn't have to.

"So what should I do?" she asked.

"What? Um... Well hon, I don't know. I think you're just going to have to learn to deal with bullies. They're going to be with you for the rest of your life."

Denise looked stunned. "It's not fair! I didn't do

anything wrong. She should be punished! Instead, I got a tardy mark and she got to laugh at me for the rest of the day!" She dropped her fork in her plate, stood up and ran from the table, tears running down her face.

"Well," said Maggie, "you handled that well."

Mark stared at her for a moment, then slowly turned back to his meal. He knew she was right, but wasn't in the mood to admit it. Both of them ate the rest of their meal in silence.

***

After dinner, Mark headed downstairs to his workshop. He was just finishing up the wings for his latest radio controlled airplane--a P51 Mustang. Working on the model took a lot of concentration. The focus required usually allowed him to put the worries of the day behind him. Unfortunately, he must have been more worried than normal. As he was trying to fit one of the struts in place, he bent the stringer too far and heard a crack.

He quickly bent down to take a look. It was ruined. He was going to have to pull all of the struts out and put in a completely new stringer. Before he knew what he was doing, he picked up the entire wing and threw it across the room. It bounced off the far wall and broke into several pieces. He was stunned. He had just completely destroyed several hours' worth of work.

"What the hell is wrong with me?" He covered his face with his hands and leaned over until his head touched the worktable. "I'm losing my mind."

He slowly got up, gingerly collected the pieces of the broken wing, and put them on the workbench. He'd look at it again later to see if he could salvage anything. Right now, he realized he needed to go and apologize to a little girl before she went to bed.

Swimming In Quicksand

He climbed the stairs and knocked on Denise's closed bedroom door.

He heard her bumping around inside. "What?"

He opened the door a crack and stuck his head into her room. She was standing at her dresser putting her earrings in one of the little compartments of her jewelry box. He sighed to himself. When had his little girl become such a pretty young lady? It was amazing how much she looked like her mother. "Can we talk?" he asked.

"Sure." Without looking at him, she crossed the room and sat on the edge of her bed.

He joined her. "I wasn't very fair to you during dinner. You had a very rough day and my comment didn't make it any better. Can we start again?"

"Sure daddy. I'd like that very much."

They spend the next 15 minutes discussing her day, her feelings about being bullied, and some strategies she might try if it ever happened again. They agreed that he would call the school tomorrow to report the incident to the office and she would go talk with her homeroom teacher. They ended with a hug and a kiss.

"I love you daddy," she said as she wrapped her arms around his neck.

"I love you, too, Girlie-Q," he responded using his favorite nickname for her. He stood up and headed for the door. "Have a good night, I'll see you in the morning." He blew her a kiss, then closed her door quietly behind him and headed toward his bedroom.

As he stepped into the bathroom, Maggie was standing at the sink brushing her hair. "Did you say goodnight to Denise?"

"Yes," he replied. "I really made her feel bad, didn't I?"

"Yes you did. Mark, you've been angry and stressed for the past few months. What's up?"

"I didn't get the job. This was the fourth one. I'm beginning to think I'll be stuck here forever."

She walked over and put her arms around him. "I'm sorry. I know it's hard, but something's got to change. We're here for you, but we can't keep this up. It's hard on all of us." She kissed him, and then turned to leave. "Now come to bed. It's been a long day, and you could use some sleep."

He finished getting ready for bed and slipped under the covers beside Maggie. "Good night," he said as he kissed her.

"Good night," she mumbled.

He stared at the ceiling. She was right. Something needed to change or he and his family were going to self-destruct. He finally rolled over and fell into a fitful sleep.

CHAPTER 3 – Hope

Mark's clock always made a quiet click right before the alarm sounded. At 5:29 he heard the click and hit the button before the alarm could wake Maggie. He was exhausted and felt like he hadn't slept at all. Still, he was determined to make it to work on time. He rubbed his eyes, eased himself out of bed, and shuffled his way to the bathroom. Thirty minutes later he was headed out the door, coffee in one hand, banana and briefcase in the other.

At this time of morning, traffic on the expressway was light and he made it to work by 6:35. Since he was early, he drove past the office and headed down the street to pick up another cup of coffee. As he pulled into the parking lot of the little coffee shop, he saw one of his former co-workers heading to the front door. He quickly parked his car and hopped out. As he jogged across the lot he called, "Is that THE Joseph Pahl? Long time, no see!"

Joe turned and smiled when he recognized Mark. "Well if it isn't Mark Johnson. How ya doin', buddy?"

"I've been better, but it isn't anything winning the lottery wouldn't cure. How's your new job going?"

Joe's smile widened. "Great! For the first time in my working life I can honestly say I look forward to getting up in the morning."

What a change. Mark thought back to a little over a year ago. He and Joe were cube neighbors and Joe certainly didn't look forward to going to work then. In fact, the two of them spent many lunch hours complaining loudly about their jobs.

Then, about nine months ago Joe changed. He stopped complaining. When Mark would launch into something he thought was wrong or unfair, Joe would just smile, make some polite excuse, and turn back to his work. Then, six months ago, Joe stepped into Mark's cube and announced he would be leaving Amalgamated to teach classes at the local university. Mark took him to lunch to congratulate him and they'd promised to keep in touch, but hadn't.

"Are you still at Amalgamated?" Joe asked.

"Yeah, but its killing me. I need to do something different. Last night, I came home and treated Maggie and Denise like crap. I don't even know why. If I don't change something, I'm afraid I might do or say something stupid and lose them."

"I hear you," said Joe. "Remember? I was there, too. Right before Christmas last year, I blew up at my boys because they were—get this—'too damn happy.' And it wasn't just that. Everything was going badly. I dreaded getting up on week days. Katherine and I were fighting over the silliest things. Most nights I couldn't sleep. The fact is, I felt trapped. I hated what I was doing but couldn't quit because I had bills to pay. I tried to keep things to myself, but my frustration at work kept bleeding into the relationship with my wife and kids. I was hurting the people I loved the most. After the fifth yelling match with Katherine, I knew I needed to make major changes or I'd lose her and the boys."

Mark leaned toward Joe. "What did you do? How did you make it work?"

Swimming In Quicksand

"It wasn't easy. Trying to find a new job after 10 years at Amalgamated was scary. At first, I couldn't decide what to do. Once I decided I wanted to teach, I wasn't sure if I could. That first job interview was really tough."

"Joe, I'm in exactly the same position you were. I need to do something or I'm going to self-destruct. Is there any way we could talk more about this? I'd love to hear how you discovered what you wanted to do, how you found the courage to take that first step, how you brought your family along, and anything else you think helped make your change successful."

"Hmmmm..." Joe thought for a minute. "You know, I think I can do better than that. How about if I introduce you to my coach, Steve?"

"Your coach?"

"Yep. Would you be interested?"

Mark didn't have to think for long. "If this guy helped you I'd love to meet him. What did you say his name was?"

"Steve." Joe smiled. "I'll tell you what. I still get together with Steve occasionally, just to keep in touch. We're supposed to meet for lunch tomorrow. Would that work for you?"

Mark pulled out his smartphone and glanced at his calendar. "Yeah. That works for me."

Joe suggested a new place, Maribelle's. "The food is very good, and they have tables where we can easily carry on a conversation." He also suggested 11:30 to make certain they avoided the rush.

Mark shook Joe's hand and smiled. "Thanks buddy! I'll see you tomorrow."

He smiled all the way back to his car, and was humming to himself as he pulled into his parking spot at work. It wasn't until around 10:30 that he realized he'd forgotten to get coffee. "Oh well," he thought, "Who needs coffee when you've got a new attitude?"

It ended up being the best day he'd had at work for a very long time.

CHAPTER 4 – Introductions

Mark arrived at Maribelle's at 11:15. He hadn't slept well the night before, and the morning seemed to last forever. At 11, he gave up trying to be productive and left for the restaurant. He had to admit he was nervous. He didn't know what to expect but felt like he was heading for a job interview.

The first thing Mark noticed about Maribelle's was the color. The outside of the building was a sunny yellow with light orange accents. It looked bright and cheery. The building was relatively small and square, and the front was dominated by two very large windows with southwestern looking wooden frames. As Mark pulled in, he noticed the parking lot was more than half full. "Looks like Joe wasn't kidding about the lunch rush," he thought to himself.

The second thing he noticed was the aroma. As he opened his car door his mouth began to water. Even from across the parking lot he could smell grilling meat, hot corn chips, and the zing of a good salsa. "Wow! If it tastes half as good as it smells, I'm going to be in culinary heaven."

As he walked through the front door, he was again taken by the colors. The sunlight streaming through the many windows landed on light reds, oranges, and yellows. Mark also noticed bright blues and greens here and there. Along the back wall was a mural depicting a town square complete with a fountain. The bright colors and simple style made Mark smile. It just felt happy.

"Can I help you?" said a cheery voice.

He turned toward the cash register stand and saw an attractive young lady with long black hair. Her brown eyes sparkled, and her smile seemed to light up the room. "Ummm... Yeah, I'm supposed to meet a couple of people for lunch."

"Would they be Joe and Steve?" she asked.

"They sure would. Did they make a reservation?"

"Not really," she answered, "It's just their regular day for lunch, and they usually arrive at 11:30, on-the-button." She glanced at her watch. "You beat them here by about ten minutes." She walked around the register stand, holding three menus. "Follow me, and I'll show you to their regular table."

As Mark followed, he continued to look around the room. The place was very clean and cheery with about 10 tables spaced around the middle of the room and several booths evenly spaced around the walls. Most of them were occupied by people engaged in lively conversations. Every table had a brightly colored Mexican village themed mosaic on top; women hanging laundry, men working on a building, children playing. He smiled again. He was going to have to bring Maggie here. She'd love it.

The young lady stopped at a booth in the back corner, next to a window. Mark noticed the mosaic was of a school house.

"Here you go," she said, placing the menus on the table. She then turned and held out her hand. "By the way, I'm Maribelle. Welcome. I know you'll enjoy both the food and the conversation. Steve and Joe are great guys."

"You're the owner?"

"Yes sir. As well as hostess, head waitress, chief cook, and bottle washer. I'll be back in a moment with some chips and salsa. Make yourself comfortable."

Mark sat down, and within a couple of minutes Maribelle returned with a full tray. She quickly set a pitcher of water, three glasses, a basket of chips that smelled fresh out of the oven, and three dishes of salsa on the table.

"Wow, three different types of salsa!" he said. "How do I know which to try?"

Maribelle smiled and pointed to each dish as she described them. "'Wimpy', 'Spicy but Irresistible', and 'Ay Carrumba! But it's a good kinda hurt!'." She laughed at the look on his face as she described the last one. "I'd recommend starting with 'Wimpy' and working your way up as you get more comfortable. With a flip of her tray, she headed back into the kitchen.

He only had a chance to try 'Wimpy' before Joe and someone else walked through the front door. Mark waved to catch their attention. Joe's companion was a gentleman of medium height and build. His head was completely bald except for a thin ring of short brown hair just above his ears. What really caught Mark's attention was the man's smile. It stretched from ear-to-ear and lit up his whole face. As both walked toward the booth, the man said hello to several people and shook several hands. He seemed to be well known and well liked.

Joe reached the table first and made introductions. "Glad you could make it, buddy! Mark Johnson, I'd like to introduce you to Stephen Trenner."

As Mark stood, Steve reached out and gave a warm and firm handshake. "Please, call me Steve. I'm very glad to meet you."

As they sat down, Maribelle instantly appeared. "What can I get the three of you?"

Steve laughed. "I think I'll have The Usual."

"Me too, " said Joe laughing, too.

"What is the usual and what's the joke?" asked Mark smiling.

"Well," Maribelle said laughing, "They order the Chicken Chimi and a diet soda every time. To honor them, I've listed it in my lunch menu as 'The Usual'."

"Excellent!" said Mark laughing now, too. "That sounds delicious. I'll have 'The Usual', too."

"A fine choice," she answered and headed back to the kitchen.

While they waited for their meal, they discussed small things. Mark learned Steve was a rabid Chicago Bears fan and was miserable because they weren't doing very well. Once their food arrived, they began discussing the weather and the economy.

As they finished up their meal, Steve asked Mark what he did. Mark said he'd been in Information Technology for about twelve years. He started at the company Help Desk, but soon began working on programming projects. He told Steve his current position was the Lead of a team of web application developers who focused on front-end applications for Amalgamated.

Mark paused and took a deep breath. "However, I'd like to be a manager within my division and think I'd be good at it. Unfortunately, leadership doesn't seem to agree. I've been passed over, twice, and have been 'the other candidate' for four other positions"

"How frustrating," said Steve. "Do you know why?"

"Not really." Mark shrugged. "They made comments about wanting someone with more large-project management experience, but that was all I could learn. I'm sure my recent performance has started to suffer. My morale has certainly taken a dive. My wife, daughter, and friends have noticed it. So, I can't help but believe it's showing up in my work performance, too."

Joe nodded in agreement. "It was the same for me."

Steve held his hand up. "It's actually pretty common, and often manifests as a self-defeating spiral." His finger made a descending spiral as he spoke. "You want something badly, but fail to get it. You become upset and question your skills. Your morale and confidence drop. Your performance suffers. You try again, and this time you do worse." His finger spiraled some more. "Pretty soon, you feel trapped. In fact, for many people, it seems the harder they try the worse things get. I call it 'drowning in quicksand'."

Mark nodded. "That is exactly how I feel. No matter what I try, things just keep getting worse. It feels hopeless."

"Oh, it's not," reassured Steve. "There are lots of ways to get out of the trap. Just like with quicksand, the trick is to use the right techniques rather than expending all your energy thrashing around. Sometimes all you need is a different perspective and a little help."

"Is that what you do, teach people how to swim, instead of drown, in quicksand?" asked Mark.

Steve's eyes lit up. "Swimming in quicksand. I like that. Do you mind if I steal it?"

Mark smiled, enjoying the conversation. "Not at all."

Steve continued. "That's exactly what I do. I teach people how to swim in quicksand. I use my experience, interviewing, and occasionally some tools to help folks make plans to improve their current situation. I try to help them discover what drives them, clarify and narrow their list of possibilities, and create an actionable plan. Then, I hold them accountable for implementing that plan."

"Can't people do that by themselves?" asked Mark.

"Some can. However, occasionally we all need a little help." Steve leaned in and lowered his voice. "I'll tell you a secret. I do this for a living, now, but the reason I got interested was because I was in a situation much like yours. Looking back, I can see that I was the largest reason things were deteriorating. Back then it felt like everyone was conspiring against me. I went to a friend for help and was introduced to an executive coach--Nancy. I was so impressed with Nancy I decided to learn more about coaching. The rest is history."

Joe chimed in. "Good thing, too." He turned to Mark. "I think I'd still be at Amalgamated if I hadn't met Steve. Our conversations encouraged me to explore what interested me and clarify what I really wanted. His prodding and suggestions enabled me to create actionable plans. However, what helped me the most was his ability to keep me honest and on target. There were several times when I think I would have quit if it hadn't been for Steve's support."

Steve smiled. "Thanks Joe, but you did all the work. I only provided a second pair of eyes, and asked you questions to keep you on track. You see Mark, humans are notorious for our ability to believe that what we hear in our head is the truth. One of the jobs of a coach is to offer other viewpoints and point out when a client might be taking his or her own opinions too seriously."

"So if you and I were going to work together, what would be our next steps?" asked Mark.

Steve bent down to rummage in the courier bag he had stashed at his feet. "I think the first step would be to get to know each other a little better. Here's a packet that contains information about me, and some questions for you. Why don't you read through it, and take a shot at answering the questions. Once you have, if you are still interested, we can get together to discuss your answers and where we might go from there."

Mark glanced at his watch. "Oh my! I really need to get

going. I had no idea we've been talking for over an hour." Jumping up, he reached for his wallet.

"Shoo! Go!" said Joe, waving his hand. "I'll get this one. You can buy me lunch next time we get together."

"You sure, Joe?" asked Mark.

"Yes, now go."

Mark shook hands with both of them, thanked Joe for lunch, and headed out of the restaurant. When he reached his car, he caught himself humming again. Two days in a row. He smiled, started his car and headed to work.

CHAPTER 5 – Things Are Looking Up

Mark's good mood carried him through the rest of the afternoon. While his schedule indicated six meetings during the remaining four hours of the day, time seemed to fly by. Before he knew it, he was grabbing his jacket and heading for the door. As he was getting into his car, he realized he was humming again. It felt good to leave work happy.

This time he remembered traffic was likely to be bad on the expressway and headed through town instead. While it was stop-and-go, it still only took fifteen minutes longer than his morning drive. As he pulled into the driveway, he checked his watch and saw it was only 5:50. He hopped out of the car and headed into the house, gently pressing the garage door switch on his way in.

Maggie and Denise were just setting the table for dinner. "You're home!" Maggie said, reaching out to give him a hug and kiss.

"I certainly am," Mark answered, "and I'm also very happy to see my two favorite ladies." He returned Maggie's hug and gave Denise a quick kiss on the cheek. "Let me wash up and I'll be right down for dinner."

Denise turned to grab the napkin holder and place it on the table. "Perfect timing Daddy. Mommy and I decided we wanted pizza tonight and it will be done in just a few minutes."

"Mmmmmm... That sounds great. I'll be right back to help set the table." Mark headed into the study, dropped off his things, then headed upstairs to wash up. When he returned, the three of them continued setting the table. They finished just as the timer rang.

"Let's eat. I'm starved," Mark said as he sat down.

Maggie finished cutting the pizza and brought it to the table.

"Can I serve?" asked Denise.

"Absolutely," answered Maggie. "By the way, Denise has something to tell you."

Denise picked up the spatula from the table and scooped a slice of pizza on to Mark's plate. "I got an 'A+' on my history project!" She was so excited she was bouncing up and down in her chair.

"Which project was that?" asked Mark.

"The 'King Tut' project! Remember, the one where I made the model of his burial chamber and wrote the paper about the discovery of his tomb?"

"That's wonderful, sweetie! I am very proud of you. I know you worked hard on that project. You deserved a good grade."

"Thanks Daddy," she said, beaming.

Maggie also had a good day. She and a colleague had put together a proposal they believed would reduce billing errors for her company. The two of them had presented it to management right after lunch. The presentation had gone well. The proposal was accepted and they were put in charge of the team assigned to roll the plan out to the rest of the department. It was a huge honor. As Maggie described it, Mark could see how pleased she was.

When everyone finished eating, they chased Denise

upstairs to finish her homework while they cleaned up.

As Maggie carried the stack of plates from the table to the sink she said, "It looks like you had a good day, too. This has been the most pleasant evening we've had in over a month."

"I know, hon. And you're right. I had a very good day. The friend Joe introduced me to was great. He called himself a coach. I'm still not quite sure what that is, but our meeting got me energized and excited."

He continued. "I know I haven't been very much fun to be around lately, but I sure hope to change that." He leaned over and kissed her on the cheek. "Meeting with this guy today made me feel like there are all kinds of possibilities."

After the table was cleared, Maggie headed into the living room to watch some television, and Mark headed to the office.

He sat down and pulled out the papers Steve had given him. Written at the top was "Pre-Coaching Questionnaire", followed by several questions. Mark read through them. "Wow," he thought, "these are tough." He reached for a pen and started working his way through them. What are your values? What are your passions? What drives you or moves you? What are you feeling in your job today? Why do you believe you feel that way? When was the last time you felt satisfied at work? What were you doing? What was the atmosphere? Why do you believe it was satisfying? What parts of your job do you like? Do you have other activities you find interesting and energizing? Do you know what you would like to do differently? By the time he finished writing, it was nearly Denise's bed time. His hand was a little cramped, but he felt pretty good. He'd been able to answer all of the questions.

Before he forgot, he grabbed his phone and thumbed a quick email to the address Steve had given him. Just before he hit the send button he read through it.

"Steve,

I just finished the pre-coaching questionnaire. Meeting with you today, and thinking about these questions has me excited about starting. I would love to meet with you at your earliest convenience.

Mark."

Satisfied that auto-correct hadn't done anything embarrassing, he touched the send button and headed upstairs to tuck Denise into bed. As he turned off the lights in the office, he realized he was in a great mood. He smiled and shook his head. "I could get used to this."

CHAPTER 6 – The Overview

The next morning Mark awoke before his alarm, again. However, this morning he felt rested and ready to go. He hopped out of bed and started to get ready for work. Denise was also up and ready to go quickly. He walked her to the end of the driveway and they talked about her plans for the day while they waited for her bus. When the bus came he kissed her goodbye, waved as the bus pulled away, and headed for his car.

He was headed out of the driveway by 7:10. Traffic was light and he pulled into the parking lot just as the dashboard clock changed to 7:45. He smiled to himself. Being at work on time twice didn't make it a habit. Even so, he felt like he was headed in the right direction.

As he walked into his office his cell phone rang. He pulled the phone out of his pocket. "Hello, this is Mark."

"Hey there Mark. Steve here. Sorry to call so early, but I got your email and wanted to let you know someone canceled and I have time on my calendar today. "

"Excellent!" said Mark as he sat down at his desk and started to sign into his computer. "What time?"

"Well, most of my clients like to meet for about 90 minutes. If that length seems okay, would three this afternoon work?"

Swimming In Quicksand

Mark double-clicked to open his calendar. His cursor changed to an hourglass, and he drummed his fingers on the table as he waited to see his schedule. "Ummmmm... Sorry.... My computer is being slow..." His calendar finally opened and he noticed it was completely empty after 2pm. He quickly scheduled himself as busy. "That works great for me. Where should we meet?"

"Where would you feel comfortable? I could give you directions to my office, or if you have someplace you feel comfortable, I'd be willing to come to you?"

Mark thought for a second. "How about Maribelle's? It seemed to work before."

"That works for me. We're both familiar with it, and at three it should be nearly empty and quiet enough for us to talk. Even better, if we're really nice, Maribelle may refill our diet soda and chips all afternoon." He laughed. "Oh, and I almost forgot, could you fax or email your questionnaire? It would be helpful to see it before our meeting."

"I can. I'll scan and email it right away," said Mark, "and I'll see you at Maribelle's at three this afternoon!"

"Perfect. See you then."

Mark punched the end button, and sat back in his chair, smiling. He could hardly wait.

***

Mark pulled into the parking lot and glanced at the dashboard clock. 2:55. There were plenty of spaces so he parked close to the front door. After locking his car he walked into the restaurant.

Maribelle looked up and smiled. "Welcome back! Steve is already here. He's sitting at the same table as yesterday." She leaned in conspiratorially. "He always sits there. It's his favorite. I think he likes the mosaic."

As Mark reached the table, Steve stood up to shake his hand. "Good to see you. I'm glad we could make this work today. When I got your note and saw the cancellation, I figured the sooner the better."

"This worked out great," said Mark as they both sat down. "I'm very excited to get started. How do we begin?"

"Well, why don't I tell you a little more about myself and how I work?"

Steve began by explaining he had been a full-time coach for the past five years. Before that, he was a mid-level manager for one of the larger firms in the city. "I really thought I wanted to be a manager, but once I moved up a couple of rungs, I realized something was missing. I was spending all of my time in meetings and had very little opportunity to meet one-on-one with my staff. One of the things I enjoyed most was helping people realize their career goals, and my job didn't allow much of that."

He began by canceling any meetings he could, and replaced them with one-on-one meetings with his staff. Soon after, several of his staff began gaining excellent reputations throughout the organization. It wasn't long before other managers were approaching him to ask his secret and if he could meet with their staff, too. After a year of part-time coaching within his company and helping members of his church, he had developed enough of a reputation that one of the local colleges asked if he would work with their students. They even offered to pay him.

Shortly after that, he decided to coach full-time. After researching what that would take, he sought out education, became certified, set up his practice, and never looked back.

Steve mentioned he used a five-step coaching model called the five "O"s. The "O"s stood for Overview, Objectives, Options, Operations, and Obstacles.

Steve suggested they might start with the overview. The

purpose would be to discuss Mark's current situation, to learn who Mark was, what he wanted, and what he believed was keeping him from succeeding.

Once they had explored Mark's current situation, Steve thought they should talk about goals and objectives. The two of them would explore where Mark wanted to go and what he might need to accomplish to get there.

The next step would be for the two of them to brainstorm what knowledge, skills, and experiences would be necessary to accomplish Mark's objectives.

During the next step, they would take the options and create operational tasks from them.

Mark stopped Steve, "What do you mean by operational tasks?"

"We'll create a list of things for you to accomplish. However, it will be more than just a to-do list. To make the tasks operational, we'll discuss not only what needs to be done, but also when you think it will be done, and how you know it's done."

"Okay..." Mark replied.

"Quite frankly," said Steve, "operations might be the most important 'O'. Unfortunately, it's also where most people struggle. Making plans is easy. However, if a person isn't able to turn those plans into action, the plan is wasted. As I like to say, 'a plan without action isn't worth squat!'"

Steve went on to explain that after they had operational tasks, they would explore any obstacles Mark might experience, and see how they might adjust their plans to either eliminate or reduce them.

Finally, Steve told Mark that once they had the initial planning out of the way, Mark would need to "do, review, rinse, and repeat." When Mark looked confused, Steve chuckled and explained that coaching was a cyclic process. The basic tenet is to make some well-planned changes, see how they work, use the results to plan for the next steps, and keep doing this until you reach the outcome you want.

Steve cautioned, "I do need to say that once the plan is in place, it will be up to you to do the work. The two of us will take time at each meeting to review how things are going, and I'll be holding you accountable for achieving whatever results we agreed upon during the previous meeting. You will always have the final say on whether you believe the results are moving you in the right direction. If you don't like what happened, we'll work to find a way to improve it next time. But, for any changes to occur, you need to commit to getting the work done."

"Sounds simple enough," said Mark sarcastically as Steve leaned back to stretch.

Steve smiled. "I know it sounds complex, but once we get into it, you'll see that it's really pretty simple. There isn't any rocket science here. Most people fail for one of two reasons. They either have no plan and jump into activity after activity, or they spend all their time planning and never take any action. Our aim is to avoid both. To help with that, I'll ask you to assign yourself some kind of homework for every session. I've found creating mini-goals and action steps will not only get you there faster, but will help you stay motivated. It also gives you an opportunity to reflect on your answers, actions, and outcomes. That self-reflection is very important and can lead to new ideas and discoveries."

"That sounds really good," said Mark. "So, how much will this cost?"

"Well, I prefer not to think of it as cost but rather an investment in your career. With that in mind, here is a sheet that discusses options, plans, agreements, and fees."

They spent a few more minutes discussing options, timelines, and plans. After several questions, Mark was able to identify a plan that seemed to work for him.

"Excellent. We've made our first step," said Steve. "Do you have any other questions?"

"Yup. When do we start?" asked Mark.

"How about now?" Then Steve paused. "I almost forgot. Before we begin, I'd like to talk about confidentiality. It is critical you feel comfortable. I promise that I will assume anything you say to me is confidential unless you tell me otherwise. I would also like to ask if you mind if I take notes while we talk. It helps me remember what you've said, and any ideas that might occur to me. As I mentioned, I promise not to share them with anyone without your explicit permission."

Mark smiled. "That works for me."

Steve opened up a legal pad and uncapped his pen. "Then, why don't we start our overview? Let's start with your questionnaire answers. Then, I'd love to hear more about what you're experiencing right now and what you'd like to accomplish."

Steve pulled his copy of Mark's questionnaire out of his bag and during the next half-hour they reviewed Mark's answers. Then, Mark spoke about his background, his current position, what he enjoyed, what he disliked, where he believed he wanted his career to go, and why. They also spent time talking about where Mark felt he was successful, and what he believed to be his strengths.

As they finished, Steve jotted a couple more notes then looked up. "So, to summarize, it sounds like you've been in your current position for eight years. You really want new challenges. You enjoy getting to know your colleagues, working one-on-one with team members, and watching them succeed. You feel at your best when the team is working well and get excited when ideas and deliverables are flowing. You love it when people stop by just to visit. Right now, a move into full-time management is appealing. The position doesn't have to be within Amalgamated, but you'd prefer it to be. Until today, you'd assumed leading a unit within your current division would be the best fit, but you are willing to explore opportunities elsewhere, too. Did I catch everything?"

"I think so."

"Excellent!" Steve tapped his legal pad with his pen. "You know, the one thing I don't remember talking about was why you haven't been able to move forward. What do you think might be getting in your way?"

After thinking for a moment, Mark mentioned he really hadn't gotten much feedback from the interviewers. In all three cases, they told him he had interviewed well. The only useful information he received was from the last interview. The hiring manager had told him they had chosen another candidate because that individual seemed to have more large-project experience.

"Well that's a place to start, but this seems important enough to warrant further investigation. Let's do some quick brainstorming. What could you do, or who could you ask to better understand what might be holding you back?"

Mark was able to come up with several ideas. "Well, I could ask my supervisor to provide input. I could also ask co-workers or team members what they thought might be keeping me from becoming a manager." After a moment of thoughtful silence he added, "It might also be interesting to talk with one of the folks on the interview panel to see if they had more specific feedback."

Steve finished writing and glanced up. "Are there any ideas we've listed you would feel comfortable doing in the next week or two?"

"Well," said Mark slowly, "I could easily talk to my supervisor. We have a pretty good relationship and he'd be willing to help me.

"Good!" said Steve. "Anything else?"

Mark looked at the list. He thought about asking a couple of his friends at work, and perhaps his administrative assistant. "My administrative assistant works with several managers. Maybe I'll ask if there are things they do habitually that I don't."

"That is an excellent thought. Do you think you could do both of them in the next few days?"

Mark paused to think. "I might be able to. But with my schedule this week, I'm not confident I could get both done. Could we start with just one?"

"Which one do you think would give you the most information?"

"Talking with my supervisor would probably give me the most information and the most benefit. It's also the one I feel the most comfortable trying."

Steve smiled. "Works for me. So, if I heard correctly, within the next few days, you should be able to have a chat with your supervisor to see if he can help you discover what might be holding you in your current position. Can I write that down as something you'll do before our next meeting?"

"Sure," said Mark thoughtfully. "So, is that my homework?"

"I think so," answered Steve with a smile. "When should we meet again?"

They both pulled out their smartphones and were able to find free time the following Tuesday. In fact, they decided Tuesday afternoons at 3:30 would work great for the next few weeks.

"Will meeting this coming Tuesday still give you enough time to do your homework?" asked Steve.

Mark smiled. "I think so."

"Excellent! Then I guess we'll talk more on Tuesday. In the meantime, if you have questions or run into problems, please don't hesitate to get in touch. I'm here to help."

Steve stood and offered his hand. Mark stood and shook it, grabbed his things, and walked toward the door. Maribelle waved to him as she came out of the kitchen and headed toward one of the tables to take someone's order.

"That was fun!" Mark said to himself as he got into his car. "Even though I haven't really changed anything, I finally feel like I'm doing something.

"Wait a minute, I have changed something. I've changed my attitude." He was still smiling as he pulled into his garage and his good mood lasted the rest of the night.

CHAPTER 7 – Homework

As it turned out, Mark was able to start his homework right away. The next morning, as he walked into the office, he ran into Jeff, his supervisor. Before he could talk himself out of it, he took a deep breath and said, "Hey Jeff, would you have time this week to meet? I've been doing some thinking about my career and I'd love to ask some questions."

"Absolutely!" Jeff replied as he pulled out his phone. "Let's see, I have time tomorrow at 11. Would that be soon enough?"

Mark checked his calendar. "That works great. I'll see you then."

***

The next day at 10:55, Mark stopped by Jeff's office. The door was open, but the office looked empty. Mark poked his head in to check for Jeff and noticed the bookshelf was full. He chided himself for not noticing this before. As he read the titles, he saw that most of them were related to management. "The One Minute Manager" by Ken Blanchard, "Leadership is an Art" by Max DuPree, "The Leadership Challenge" by James M. Kouzes and Barry Z. Posner, and "Leadership and Self Deception: Getting Out of the Box" by a group called The Arbinger Institute all caught his eye. Mark had never been much of a reader, but it seemed Jeff was. Now that he thought about it, he remembered seeing books in just about every manager's office. "Hmmm... If all managers read this much, maybe I should start reading too."

As Mark was jotting down the titles of some books that caught his eye, Jeff arrived.

"Good Morning Mark. Sorry I'm a couple minutes late."

"No problem. I don't know why I didn't notice this before, but you have a lot of books."

Jeff laughed. "I do. I try to read at least one business or management book a month. I figure twelve career related books a year will help me stay at the top of my game. I also read articles and online blogs, but I've found books go deeper and give me a much better understanding of the subject." He paused. "You know, I just realized I've never asked what you like to read."

Mark paused. "To be honest, I haven't read much since college, but several of your titles caught my eye."

Jeff leaned forward eagerly. "Which ones?"

Mark mentioned a couple of titles including "The One Minute Manager."

Jeff turned, crossed to his bookshelf, pulled it out, and handed it to Mark. "This is a great little book, and it shouldn't take you very long to read. I'd love to hear what you think of it."

Mark took the book. "Wow. Thanks."

Jeff sat down at his desk and offered Mark a chair. "I could talk about books all day, but I want to be respectful of our time. If I remember correctly, you have specific questions you wanted to discuss."

Mark agreed. As he sat down, he reminded Jeff he had recently interviewed for three management positions and hadn't been offered any of them. "The first couple of times I figured I probably wasn't the right person for the job. After the third rejection, I'm feeling there must be a skill I don't have or something I'm doing that is getting in my way."

Jeff thought for a moment. "Well, I'm not aware of anything specific. After your request to meet, I did take some time to review your last couple of performance appraisals." He reached into his top desk drawer, pulled them out, and began to page through them. "Both are good. Nothing jumps out at me."

As they talked further, Jeff asked if Mark had talked with the hiring managers. Mark said he had. He found their answers polite but not very helpful. He also noted he wasn't comfortable approaching them, again, because he didn't want to seem like a poor loser.

Jeff paused and leaned back in his chair. "I don't think you'd be viewed that way. There's absolutely nothing wrong with seeking out feedback.

"However, if you've already spoken to them, I can see why it might be hard to go back. Would you mind if I spoke to them? Since they're peers, they might be willing to give me details they didn't give you. You know, I could also talk with my supervisor and some of his peers to see what they might have heard."

"That would be great!" said Mark. "I don't want to make anyone uncomfortable, I just want to know if there's something I can do to improve my chances of moving into management."

Jeff nodded. "I'll see what I can find out." He paused for a couple of seconds. "Say, if you don't have other questions, do you have a few minutes to talk about the Peterson project?"

They spoke for a few minutes about deliverables and dates, then pulled out calendars and agreed to follow-up at the end of the week.

As Mark was getting up to leave, Jeff put his pen down and looked up. "Can I ask you a question?"

"Sure."

"How come you've never asked for this type of help before? When we've had discussions about your career in the past, you've always been vague about what you wanted."

Mark thought for a moment. "Well, I've always felt unsure about asking you for help leaving the unit."

Jeff scratched his head. "Wow, that's too bad. I've always felt that part of my job was to help employees grow. Sometimes that means helping them move on. I hope discussing this type of thing won't be a problem from now on."

Mark smiled. "I hope not, too. Thank you for your help."

"You are welcome. I'll let you know what I hear."

***

On Friday afternoon, Mark got an email from Jeff mentioning he had discovered information Mark would find useful and suggesting they meet first thing Monday morning. Mark accepted the invitation thinking it would be a long weekend.

He was right. No matter how hard he tried, he couldn't stop worrying. He wasn't sure if he should be excited or nervous, so he was both. He was excited because he would hopefully learn something that could move his career forward. He was nervous because he might not like what he learned.

As soon as he got home Maggie and Denise knew something was bothering him and kept asking what it was. For most of Friday evening, Mark kept saying, "It's nothing, just some things at work." However, he knew he should tell them the truth. At breakfast on Saturday, he did. After telling them, he felt much better. While he still couldn't stop worrying about the meeting, sharing his concerns and knowing both of them were supportive made waiting a little easier.

Later that afternoon, as he straightened up his office, he noticed the book Jeff had loaned him. Maybe reading would help pass the time? He glanced out the window and noticed it was beautiful outside. "Who said reading has to be an indoor activity?" he thought. "I'm going to sit out on the deck, listen to the birds, and see what I can learn." On the way to his favorite deck chair, he stopped by the kitchen and poured himself a glass of iced tea. After stepping on to the deck, he plopped down in his chair, set his iced tea in the drink holder, and opened the book.

Before he knew it, he was halfway finished and his iced tea was empty. As he got up for a refill he thought, "Wow, I don't remember business books being that entertaining." He had the book finished by supper.

***

On Monday, he again awoke before his alarm. He looked at the clock, stretched, and hopped out of bed. Within an hour, he was pulling into the office parking lot. He parked his car and hurried to his office. He couldn't believe how excited and nervous he still was. He was so nervous he skipped his coffee for fear of appearing too jittery.

At 8am, he grabbed a tablet and "The One Minute Manager", checked to make certain he had a pen, and hurried to Jeff's office. Once there, he knocked lightly on the door frame.

Jeff looked up and smiled. "Come in, come in! How was

your weekend?"

"Good," Mark answered. He handed Jeff "The One Minute Manager". "This really helped pass the time. You were right. It was a great read and didn't take very long at all."

"Excellent!" Jeff pointed to one of the empty chairs. "Have a seat and make yourself comfortable. What did you like best about it?"

As Mark sat down, he thought for a minute. "Well, the part that spoke to me most was about setting goals, then regularly comparing behavior and performance against them. I'd like to start doing that myself and during my one on ones with the team. I think it might keep us better focused on results."

Jeff smiled. "That sounds great to me. Would you mind sharing your goals with me?"

Mark smiled a little sheepishly. "Not at all. One of the goals I'd like to set right away, is to read more books like that. Do you have any suggestions?"

"Oh, I have a couple." Jeff stood so he could better peruse his bookshelf. He grabbed two books and laid them on his desk. "Why don't you try these? They're also written as parables, but contain very useful information. I think you'll like them."

Mark picked up the books and inspected them. "Who Moved My Cheese" and "The Five Disfunctions of Teams." They looked as interesting as "The One-Minute Manager." He decided he'd start one of them as soon as he got home.

"Anyway," Jeff began, "I promised I'd talk to the managers that interviewed you and my boss to see what I might discover about your situation. As luck would have it, I was able to meet with them all by Friday afternoon. Sorry about making you wait the weekend, but I wanted a chance to organize my thoughts before we met. I think I have some very helpful information."

Mark opened his pad and took the cap off his pen. "Great. I'd love to hear what you've learned."

"Before I begin, I need to warn you, at least one of these might be hard to hear."

Mark paused, then took a deep breath. "If I don't hear them nothing will improve. So, whether I like them or not, I want to hear them all."

"I was hoping you'd see it that way."

Jeff began by telling Mark everyone had been impressed with his resume. Many of them learned several things about Mark's career, and were impressed by how much work he did outside the organization. However, in every case, there were three things that kept him from being the best candidate for the position. First, he had become invisible in his current position. Second, he didn't seem to have much experience with staff development.

Jeff took a deep breath. "Finally," he said, "they all noticed you have become less and less punctual over the past eighteen months. Everyone expressed concern it might indicate your level of commitment to the company and believed it would be a bad example for those who might report to you. As I heard them talking, I realized I've experienced it, too."

As Jeff talked, Mark felt his face flush and the muscles in his chest start to tighten. He even took a deep breath to argue with Jeff. He stopped. "Isn't this what I wanted?" he thought to himself.

Jeff stopped and looked up from his notes. "What do you think? How are you doing with this?"

Mark leaned back in his chair. "Wow." He paused and took another deep breath. "I asked for honest feedback. Can I ask some follow-up questions?"

Jeff leaned back too. "Sure."

"Let's start with the first item. What do you think they meant by 'invisible'?"

"I asked them that, too, and all of their answers were similar. Before you were a lead you were considered a 'hot-shot' programmer. You were always investigating new technologies or ways of doing things, thinking about how they might bring value, and sharing them with others. You gave presentations to other teams and organized lunchtime learning sessions. You seemed willing to do anything to help others understand what you were excited about. That energy and visibility were what made you a strong candidate for the lead position. However, once you became a lead you stopped doing those things. In fact, one manager said that until you applied for his position he thought you had left the company."

Mark thought for a moment. "That is true. Once I became a lead I began to focus on my team and what we were doing. I did drop out of the public eye." He paused to take a look at his notes. "The second one makes perfect sense. I don't have questions about it. Can we talk about the third?"

Part of Mark's concern was that he had noticed the trend, too. He had to admit his lack of career progress probably contributed. However, the largest driver was the number of meetings he was invited to attend. His calendar was packed and it was getting worse rather than better. His team was being asked to do more projects and each project seemed to require a ton of meetings.

"Do you have any suggestions about how I might address this?" Mark asked Jeff.

"Well, I do have some thoughts. However, before we talk about them, I'd like to explore any thoughts you might have. You're closer to the situation. Your thoughts are likely to be more directly applicable."

Swimming In Quicksand

Mark frowned and thought for a while. Then, he looked up. "Unfortunately, I don't."

Jeff paused for a moment, tapping his fingers on his desk and seeming to consider how he might say what was on his mind. "Do you mind if I give you some feedback?"

"No, of course not."

Jeff paused again. "I'm not sure how helpful this will be, but I've noticed you're usually on time for meetings with me. Further, you often change your schedule to facilitate mine. To me that indicates you may have more flexibility than you realize. Perhaps you need to be more ruthless in what you allow on your schedule. If you'd like, we could sit down and go through your meetings together.

"The other suggestion might be to try delegating some of your meetings. I know your team isn't excited about meetings, but it might be a good opportunity for some of them."

Mark wasn't excited about either idea, but wrote them both down. He needed to think about them more. As he was writing, he noticed that it was 8:58. "Oh my goodness! I just noticed the time. You probably have a 9 o'clock meeting."

"I do," said Jeff. He smiled. "However, they are coming to see me, so I don't have to go far."

Mark stood up. "Good. I'm glad I haven't made you late. Thank you so much for doing this, Jeff. One last question. As I think through this feedback, can I come to you if other thoughts or questions occur?"

"Absolutely, I'd be disappointed if you didn't."

Mark thanked Jeff again, and headed toward his own office. As he walked he tried to understand how he felt. On one hand, he was excited that he had made the first measurable step forward. On the other hand, the feedback regarding punctuality really bothered him.

He shrugged and willed himself to relax. While some of the feedback was unpleasant, he now had solid information. He now had an idea of where to start.

CHAPTER 8 – Objectives, Options, And Obstacles

The next afternoon, Mark arrived at Maribelle's ahead of Steve. As he walked through the door, Maribelle welcomed him back with a warm smile and told him their table was ready for them.

Steve hurried in just as Mark was sitting down. "Hey Mark." Steve reached out and patted Mark on the shoulder as he scooted around to his regular seat. "How did this week go?"

"I think it went pretty well. Not only did I get my homework done, but I learned some bonus material, too."

"Bonus material? That sounds intriguing. Tell me more."

Mark started by describing his conversation with Jeff about reading. He also told Steve about "The One Minute Manager" and how much he enjoyed the book.

"You sound surprised," Steve said.

"I am. Other than technical manuals, I don't think I've read a non-fiction book since college. I always thought they were dull. However, I liked the style of this book and I found the information useful."

Steve smiled. "Great. I'd love to hear what you learned and what you think will be most useful for us as we go forward."

"That's funny," said Mark. "Jeff asked almost the same question."

Steve laughed. "It sounds like he's a really good manager. How did you answer him?"

"Well, I told him what resonated most was the idea of creating goals, writing them down, then regularly comparing results and behaviors against what was written."

"Wonderful!" said Steve. "That lines up perfectly with the work we'll be doing. You'll get plenty of practice."

Mark nodded. "That's good because I told Jeff I wanted to do this for myself and with my team."

"Excellent. What else happened?"

Mark looked sheepish. "Well, I asked Jeff for more reading recommendations. He gave me two more books and I have to say I can't wait to start them."

Steve sat back and smiled. "Mark, this is exciting. I'm very proud of you. The most successful leaders and managers I know are continually reading to improve themselves. In fact, I like to say 'Leaders are Readers.' Welcome to the club!"

"Thank you," said Mark with a bit of a blush.

"Now, let's talk about the rest of your homework." Steve reached for his notepad and a pen. "What did you discover?"

Mark took a few moments to describe the three pieces of feedback from Jeff. Steve listened, took a few notes, and asked several questions.

Steve then put his pen down and looked over his notes. "It sounds like very constructive feedback. How do you feel about it?"

"Well," began Mark, "the first two are obviously valid. I did kind of drop off the map when I started this job. And I just haven't had much opportunity to develop my staff. While I don't have specific ideas on how to change them yet, they make sense. It's the third that bothers me."

"Tell me more," encouraged Steve.

"I feel... Well... I don't know..." Mark paused and looked at his hands, trying to decide how he might describe his feelings without whining. He couldn't think of any way to do it and could feel his face heating up.

Steve noticed Mark's discomfort. "Listen, our meetings are here for you to work through these types of issues. It looks like you have something to say, but are having a tough time. Just say it. I really don't care how it sounds, and remember, anything you say to me stays confidential. I won't tell anyone, unless you want me to. Does that help?"

"A little," Mark said. Then he took a deep breath and leaned forward. "I guess… Well… I don't want to sound like I'm whining, but it doesn't seem fair. I'm just too damn busy. I'm working my butt off." He pounded his fist on the table to emphasize his point. "I am trying to represent the team well, and all leadership sees is that I'm late for a few meetings. What am I supposed to do? I've been told our team needs to accomplish more, so I make certain our team is lined up for more projects. However, the more projects we do, the more meetings I have to attend. Now I have more meetings than my supervisor and I'm stuck. If I don't go to the meetings I'm not doing my job. If I go to the meetings I end up running late and perpetuating my reputation for tardiness. What the hell am I supposed to do?"

Steve leaned back in his chair and scratched his head. "That definitely sounds like a tricky situation. It would be easy to get stuck here. Instead, let's pause for a minute. I think we are at a point where we have a good overview, and should consider moving to the next 'O': Objectives. Let me summarize to see if I have everything.

"As we've noted before, you are definitely feeling stuck in

your current position. You've held the same position for eight years. You really want new challenges. Right now, a move into full time management is appealing. Your new opportunity doesn't have to be within your current unit or even within Amalgamated, but you'd prefer it to be. Unfortunately, there are three things holding you back. First, you've disappeared off of administration's radar. Second, there are concerns about your staff development experience. Finally, you have a reputation for being late to meetings. This might be the toughest to address, because you believe your tardiness is because you have so many meetings. Unfortunately, your meetings seem critical and you are struggling to find a way to drop some of them without being accused of not doing your job. Is that correct?"

"That just about describes things," Mark said morosely.

Steve paused briefly to collect his thoughts. "Okay, I know this seems like a tough spot, but here is where things can get interesting. In fact, I think they already have."

"How do you figure that?" asked Mark.

"Well, not only did you do a good job of creating the overview, I think we might have a good start on some objectives. It sounds to me like your homework uncovered three likely candidates." He ticked them off with his fingers as he said them. "One, become more visible to administration. Two, provide career development for your team members. Three, improve your reputation regarding punctuality. How do those feel to you?"

Mark paused to think. "Well... I guess they sound okay." He paused again. "Actually... the first two sound pretty good. I agree with the third in principle, but I'm struggling with it. I'm really struggling with it."

"Fair enough. I understand. For now, let's write them down, move forward, and see what happens." Steve took a moment to write them down. "So, which one should we work with first?"

Mark thought for a long minute. "Well, I'd really like to start by improving my reputation regarding punctuality. It's the one that bothers me the most, the one I think will be the hardest. And, I'm concerned that if I don't address it first, I won't be able to focus on the others.

"Okay... But let's take this slowly. Rather than focus on the problem, let's try to think about solutions. Let's move to the third 'O'. Let's try to create some options. If there were no issues, constraints, or as I call them, obstacles, how might you solve this problem?"

"But there are obstacles," said Mark.

"I expect there are," Steve answered. "But, worrying about them now might limit your options, unnecessarily. Sometimes we create our own obstacles, and then start to believe they are outside of our control. To ensure that isn't the case, let's pretend you're 'King for the Day'. If there were no negative consequences to you and your team what would you do to make your schedule better?"

Mark looked down at the table, obviously struggling. After a few seconds he looked up. "I'd love to drop the design meetings."

"What made you choose the design meetings?" asked Steve.

"I'm not the best designer on the team. Two other team members are much better. I think it would be better for both the team and our customers if they attended."

Steve made a note. "Okay, that's a good start. What are other meetings where others might better represent the team?"

Mark thought for a moment. "I think most of the status meetings are a waste of time. I just pass along information my staff put together. The only time I really need to participate is when a deliverable is late or there is some other emergency."

Steve nodded and wrote that idea down. "Good. Anything else?"

Mark couldn't think of anything.

"So, if you could cut out the design meetings and reduce the number of status meetings what would that do to your schedule?"

Mark thought for a moment. Dropping the design meetings and at least a third of the status meetings would free up his schedule by almost 40 percent. He mentioned that to Steve.

"Would that be enough to address your reputation for tardiness?"

"I think it would help a great deal."

Steve looked at Mark. "Okay. We've created the overview, identified some objectives, and created some options. Now, let's move to the fourth 'O'. Why can't you make those changes? What's stopping you? What are the obstacles?"

Mark sighed. "Well, our company is very meeting oriented. It's assumed if you're invited to a meeting you'll attend."

"Have you talked to your manager about this? How does he keep his calendar clean?"

Mark's cheeks reddened. "No... I haven't. I just assumed he accepted all his invitations. Now that you ask, I don't really know."

"Okay. What about the design meetings? What's keeping you from delegating them to the design experts you were telling me about?"

Mark thought about that for a minute. Most of the team regularly complained about meetings. Their mantra seemed to be that time in meetings was time wasted. However, in thinking back, he couldn't remember either of the design experts saying anything like that. In fact...

"Wait a minute Steve! I just remembered. One of the design experts mentioned to me that she'd be interested in more responsibility. I think at least one of them may be willing to try this. If she's willing and I can coach her through it, I could not only reduce the number of meetings on my calendar, but I'd also be doing staff development! Wouldn't I?"

Steve smiled. "It would seem that way to me."

Scott A. Koon

CHAPTER 9 – Maribelle's Story

The following Tuesday, Mark arrived several minutes before he and Steve were scheduled to meet. Maribelle was standing at the host stand and smiled as he walked through the door.

He waved and started to head toward their usual table, but stopped and headed back to the stand. "How is your day going?"

Maribelle laughed. "My day is going great! We had a food critic here last night and the review came out in this morning's paper." She held up a section of the local paper. "You Have To Try Maribelle's! The Best New Restaurant In Town!" was splashed across the top of the page.

"Wow! That's great!" said Mark. "Congratulations!"

"Thanks," she said. "We've been trying to get a food critic to review us for weeks. This is the last big piece of the puzzle. Now the real work begins."

"The real work?" asked Mark.

"Yup. Steve and I believed that after the local review, we would start to get really busy. Once that happened our strategy would need to change. Our initial objective was to create a smoothly working organization and we've done pretty well. However, from this point forward we'll need to step up our game. Now we need to make certain we can scale up and sustain ourselves for the long term."

"Wait," said Mark shaking his head, "You and Steve own this place?"

"What?" Maribelle laughed, again. "No, Steve is my coach too. He and I have been working together since before I opened this place." She held up the newspaper and grinned sheepishly. "Now I need his help more than ever!"

"Wow," mused Mark, "he's a busy guy."

"He is, but that's because he's so good."

"If you don't mind me asking, how long have you been working with him?" asked Mark.

"I don't mind at all," said Maribelle. "I've known Steve for about five years. We've worked on and off the whole time. I've asked him for help with several things and we typically work together for a few months at a time.

"When I first met Steve, I was an accountant for one of the larger firms in town. I'd been there for four years. The first three were really exciting. I was working with major clients and assigned to several quality teams. Things were going great. Then I got promoted and everything changed."

"What happened?" asked Mark.

Maribelle rubbed her forehead for a second. "That's the tough part. I don't really know. As part of the promotion, I moved to a new team with a new manager. The new manager welcomed me, and even took me to lunch. During that first meeting, he asked a lot of questions, described some of the challenges I would face, and asked my opinion about how to address them. It seemed like things were going great.

"The next week, I was visited by the head of the department. She also invited me to lunch and told me how excited she was to have me join the department." Maribelle leaned forward and lowered her voice. "Then things got really strange. The department chair told me she had been looking for someone like me for almost a year. My new team's productivity had been slipping for two years. Leadership suspected my supervisor was struggling and needed help. They were counting on my energy and skills to bring the team's productivity back in line with prior performance.

"At the end of lunch, she shook my hand and told me to call her if I needed anything at all." Maribelle straightened up and smiled. "When that lunch was over, I was certain I was on the fast track to the C-Suite.

"The next day, my supervisor strolled into my office and plopped down in one of my visitor chairs. After making small talk for several minutes, his demeanor changed completely. He lowered his voice and told me he was aware of my meeting with the department chair. He said I was playing a dangerous game and told me if I wanted to keep my job I'd stop trying to work around him. The more he talked, the redder his face got. By the time he finished, he was yelling and punctuating each sentence by sticking his finger in my face. Then he stopped, stood up, smiled, said he trusted I'd do the right thing, and left my office.

Maribelle crossed her arms. "I was afraid and confused. I didn't know where his concerns came from. I didn't know what to do or say. I hadn't even initiated the meeting with the department chair. She had.

Maribelle continued, "Things went from bad to worse. It didn't seem to matter what I did, I just couldn't get on my supervisor's good side. Furthermore, our bad relationship stared to impact everything I did. My work quality suffered. I started making costly mistakes, and soon I was hanging on to my job by a thread."

"What did you do?" asked Mark.

"To be honest, I was planning to leave the company. I was absolutely miserable. Every day seemed like a constant battle. The worst part was I couldn't request a transfer. Others had heard about my mistakes and nobody wanted an employee with my reputation for shoddy work.

"That's when I met Steve. He was just starting his practice and was giving a seminar at the community college entitled 'What to do when you're stuck in a dead-end job.' It was a no-nonsense look at how to put together a plan for changing or leaving."

"Is that how you decided to open the restaurant?" asked Mark.

"No. At first my plan was to fix the mess I was in. My goal was to find a way to improve my work performance, repair my reputation, and apply for a job with a different team. I found the planning was easy. Execution was a different matter.

"Based upon the information from Steve's talk, it only took me a day or two to put together what I thought was a good plan. I just never seemed to find the right opportunity to start implementing. Something would always come up, or I'd find another tweak to make.

"After about three months of getting nowhere, I contacted Steve and asked if he would meet with me. During our first two meetings, he helped me make my plan much more actionable."

Mark tilted his head to one side. "What do you mean?"

"Well, in my original plan I needed to be assigned to a project that would highlight my leadership skills. Steve helped me realize that plan was based on something I couldn't control. Instead, he encouraged me to actively seek out and volunteer for the right assignments, or find ways to change my day-to-day work to accomplish the same thing.

"As we reviewed other portions of my plan, we discovered other places where I was too risk-averse. The actions I had planned kept me employed, but wouldn't likely generate the results I wanted. I had them in the plan because I thought they were easily accomplished. I hadn't considered whether they'd move me forward or not. With Steve's help, I was able to find ways to accept more risk, create results that would stand out, and protect my job.

"The best part of working with Steve was that he never let me off the hook. He encouraged me to step outside my comfort zone, but let me create my own plan."

She shrugged. "The more I work with him, the more I realize I already have most of the answers. Sometimes, I just need a little help taking action."

Mark laughed. "Somehow I can't picture you not taking action."

Maribelle winked. "You'd be surprised. It's easy to put a plan together, but when your future is at stake taking that next step can be really hard. Steve has a saying that helped me a lot..." She stopped and smiled.

From over his shoulder, Mark heard Steve say, "A plan without action isn't worth squat!"

Mark turned to see Steve standing there with a huge smile on his face.

Steve shrugged his shoulders. "It's true. Should we see how we can turn your options into something actionable?"

"Sure," Mark turned to Maribelle. "But I need to hear the rest of your story."

Maribelle stepped from behind the podium and pushed Mark toward their usual table. "Later. I promise. Right now, you need to get to work!"

Mark groaned. All three laughed as Mark and Steve headed toward their customary table.

Swimming In Quicksand

CHAPTER 10 – The Operational Plan

Over the course of the meeting, Steve and Mark moved to the last 'O'. To create Mark's operational plan they used brainstorming and information gathered from earlier meetings. As Maribelle had mentioned, this was where Steve's help was invaluable.

They began with the list of objectives: To become more visible to administration, to provide career development to his team members, and to improve Mark's reputation regarding punctuality. For each, Steve asked Mark to consider the options brainstormed earlier and challenged him to break them into smaller and smaller steps until discrete actions were identified. Then Steve pressed Mark to answer who would do what actions by what date. To ensure the greatest likelihood of success, they worked to structure the tasks so that Mark was the one responsible for completing them. Finally, they documented all of their work.

As the 90 minutes came to a close, Mark leaned back and stretched. He couldn't believe how much they had accomplished. Before today, he felt he had been dabbling with small changes. Now he was preparing something larger and more visible. He was becoming more and more excited.

As Mark reviewed his notes, he realized the plan could be

divided into three sections. He mentally reviewed them.

First, before their next meeting Mark would make a list of his team members and their interests and talents. Then, he would brainstorm new opportunities to use those skills. Once completed, he and Steve would review the results to ensure completeness and see if they sparked other ideas.

Second, Mark would ask the two design experts to represent the team at design meetings, and bring questions or architectural decisions back to the rest of the team.

Third, Mark would ask a couple of the project managers if he could submit written updates instead of attending every project meeting. To make that possible, he would work with his team to create a one-page template for weekly status reports. He would proof the reports, add comments if necessary, and submit the reports directly to the project managers. He would assure the project managers that if he found surprises, he would attend that meeting.

Steve had been very helpful during this portion of the planning. He agreed with the concept, but pressed Mark to identify specific project managers, by name, and identify a date by which the conversations would occur. Further, he asked Mark to clarify if the whole team would create the template or if it would be created by a subset and endorsed by the team. When Mark decided it would be created by one or two members of the team, Steve pressed for names and times.

As usual, Mark was amazed by how helpful Steve's questions and suggestions were. He felt so smart when they worked together. Steve had a knack for asking just the right question to keep things on track. More than once, Mark started a session by describing how badly a day had gone, or how irritating an individual was. Steve would let Mark talk for a while, then smile and ask how that was related to what they were trying to accomplish. While Mark was embarrassed to be caught whining, he was pleased to note that even those conversations sparked valuable ideas.

What amazed Mark most was that the plan was all his. Steve kept conversations productive and helped clarify ideas or tasks. However, the ideas, answers, and decisions all came from Mark. It appeared that Steve not only knew how to move things along, but he knew when to get out of the way too.

During one of their meetings, Mark asked Steve, "Why does it seem so easy when we work together?"

Steve sat back and smiled. "If I gave away my secrets how would I make a living?" He paused. "Seriously, though, the success we've had boils down to a couple of things. First, you really want to improve and have opened yourself to feedback. Never underestimate the power of passion. Second, you're good at what you do. My contributions were to ask questions to help you discover your own path, give you an unbiased opinion, and hold you to your commitments."

Steve made it sound simple, but Mark wasn't so sure. It was so easy to talk with Steve that there had to be some magic involved. He thought about digging deeper but saw Steve looking at him from across the table. He shrugged, smiled, and returned to the operational plan.

CHAPTER 11—Implementation

After weeks of planning, it was finally time to execute. Mark began by meeting with his team. He already had one-on-one meetings with each of his staff, so he used those to explore skills and discuss opportunities they might be seeking. Before the meetings, Mark thought he knew his team fairly well. However, he was surprised by several things.

First, he learned the two designers were very excited about attending design meetings for the team. He had underestimated their desire for more challenging work. Both were proud of their skills and believed this would give them new opportunities to help out.

Besides agreeing to attend the meetings, one of them offered to create a document listing the team's standard design strategies and the advantages and disadvantages of each. The other volunteered to review upcoming project requests and let Mark know if any might impact the team. Within a week, both ideas were integral parts of the team's process.

Clearly, Mark had overestimated the team's reluctance to attend meetings. Past conversations led him to believe this might be a difficult topic. During conversations with the designers and other members of the team, he learned most of them welcomed the opportunity to represent the team. What concerned them was the possibility that meetings might become such a large part of their workday they would miss delivery dates, their skills would erode, or both. As Mark visited with individuals, each happily agreed to attend one or two meetings as long as there was a way to revisit assignments should the workload become overwhelming.

Finally, Mark learned one of his team members loved puzzles. Bill solved at least one Sudoku puzzle every morning on his bus ride to work. Not only did it pass the time, but he believed it kept his mind sharp.

Mark thought about how hard it was to create the weekly schedule. The challenge was to move projects forward without overextending anyone. It took days to find the right balance. He hated it.

As Mark described his struggles, Bill asked if he could take a look at it. Mark happily agreed.

Later that afternoon Bill stopped by to ask Mark's opinion regarding a first draft. Mark was amazed. In a couple of hours Bill had created a nearly perfect schedule.

Unfortunately, before they could show the team, someone stopped by with a conflict. Mark hated trying to adjust for these last minute changes, but Bill smiled and rubbed his hands together. Within 30 minutes a new schedule was on Mark's desk. On top of the schedule was a note.

"Thanks for the challenge. I really enjoyed helping you with the schedule. Let me know if there are other changes you need. Thanks, Bill."

Mark also noticed improvements in his relationship with Jeff. Mark finished several book suggestions, and found that Jeff loved to talk about them. Their new conversations were much different than the transaction-based interactions they used to have. In fact, Jeff even stopped by Mark's office to talk about using ideas from an article to resolve a long-standing problem. It felt good to be consulted.

Changes were happening elsewhere, too. As part of his plan, Mark met with each of the project managers to ask what information they needed and how to best present it. Mark learned they were hungry for any information they could get. Further, they didn't care how the information arrived. They were much more interested in getting it early-- the earlier the better. The reason many of them insisted on face-to-face meetings was because of the difficulty of getting timely information.

Mark showed the project managers the one-page template his team had created. It started with an overall status and a brief summary of work done since the last update. The next section described upcoming tasks and identified those that might be at risk. The report ended with a description of deliverables and significant accomplishments. While each report was only a page long, Mark was confident it provided more information than the current, verbal reports. The project managers agreed, suggesting only a couple of formatting changes to allow the document to be used as part of their existing workflow. Once the form had been used a few times, several of the project managers were so excited they asked if they could use it for other projects.

The more Mark thought about it, the more amazed he became. In just a few weeks, so much had changed. He was feeling better about his job. He was sleeping better at night and feeling less stressed during the day. While walking back from a meeting, two of his team members mentioned how relaxed he looked. When they asked what had changed, he just smiled and quoted Steve.

"If I gave away my secrets how would I make a living?"

CHAPTER 12 – The Test

On Monday, Mark arrived at the office twenty minutes early. Maggie, Denise, and he had spent the weekend out-of-town and he was feeling rested and ready to go. This morning, he was scheduled to meet with one of the project managers and wanted to put together a quick update. He smiled as he locked his car and headed into the building. It was amazing how much better things seemed. In fact, this weekend he had come to the conclusion that he actually enjoyed his job. He still wanted to be in management, but he no longer needed to escape his current position.

He walked to his office, turned on the light and started his computer. He glanced at his phone and noticed the message light blinking. As he sat down a new email caught his eye. It was from one of the project managers, asking to call as soon as he arrived. "Hmmm, I wonder what she needs?" he thought as he began to dial her number.

The phone rang once and she picked it up. "This is Diane."

"Diane, this is Mark. What can I do for you?"

"Mark, you have a big problem! According to your updates we were on track for the Pliny project."

Mark could tell she was furious. He reached over for his

project notes and quickly flipped to the Pliny project. "According to my team things have been moving along and we should have provided deliverables last Friday. What's wrong?"

As Diane continued, her voice was shaking. "We. Got. Nothing. No code, no deliverables, and no explanation."

Mark could feel a lump forming in his stomach. "What?" he asked.

Diane continued. "As you said, we were expecting the deliverables from your team on Friday so the customer could test this weekend, but we got nothing. Neither the customer liaison nor I could reach your on-call person until this morning. When I finally spoke to James, he told me—as if this happens all the time—that they ran into a couple of problems and just weren't ready to deliver. When I asked for the new timeline he told me it would take what it took.

"That is not an acceptable answer, especially when previous status updates gave no indication of any issues or delays. When I mentioned that, he told me to back off. In fact, I think his exact words were 'I'm the technical specialist. When you know as much as I do you can tell me what to do. In the meantime, do your little job and let me get back to work.' Then he hung up on me.

Diane lowered her voice. "So, here's the bottom line. You and your team have exactly four hours to deliver something. If you don't, Pliny will invoke the non-deliverable clause in our Statement Of Work and there will be severe financial repercussions. I will also have to escalate this to our Chief Information Officer so he can ensure this doesn't permanently damage our relationship. Further, regardless of the outcome, I am filing a formal complaint against James. I want him off this project immediately. I never want to work with him again. Finally, I'm done with your little experiment. Your written reports led me to believe things were on track and working nicely. They weren't. We need to go back to our weekly face-to-face meetings. Do you have any questions?"

Mark was stunned. "Ummm... No." He looked at his watch. "By my watch, you are expecting a delivery by noon. Is that correct?"

"Before would be better, but noon will suffice."

"What is the minimum you need?"

Diane's voice turned icy. "Mark, I don't think you understand. The customer was expecting the deliverables last Friday. We need everything we were supposed to have on Friday delivered by noon. Call me, hourly, with updates. Goodbye."

The line went dead.

Mark sat back, his head spinning. What was he going to do?

"Stop!" he told himself. "I know exactly what to do." He grabbed a pad of paper and started making a list. Quick follow-up with James. Gather the team. Arrange a conference room for the day. Notify Jeff and set up a regular update schedule. At the bottom of the page, he wrote "Things to do after crisis is complete". Under that he wrote "Speak with James", "Contact HR", and "Follow-up with Diane". He took his pad and pen and headed out of his office.

***

Mark found James at his desk. "James, do you have a minute?"

James smiled. "Sure, Boss"

"I just got off the phone with Diane, the project manager for the Pliny project. She told me we didn't get the deliverables to them on Friday. Further, she said you insulted her and she wants you off the project. What happened?"

James lowered his voice. "She's quite a piece of work, isn't she? She had the gall to tell me that I had to get the deliverables done today. She has no idea what that would take."

Mark shrugged his shoulders. "What will it take?"

"It's going to take at least a week, maybe more."

Mark took a deep breath to calm himself and held up the most recent project report James had submitted. "Last Thursday you told me things were on track and we'd be handing over the deliverables as planned. What happened?"

James shrugged. "This is my week on-call and I ended up getting involved in another project. When I gave you my update on Thursday, I thought I could get the Pliny stuff done in a day. I was wrong. No big deal."

Mark felt his face starting to heat up. "Actually, it is a big deal. A very big deal. Right now, I'm gathering the team in the conference room. We have until noon to put together Friday's deliverables. If we don't deliver, things will go badly for our team. I need everyone ready to go in 15 minutes."

"Whatever you say, boss."

Fifteen minutes later, he had briefed Jeff, and he and several of the team were sitting in the conference room with their laptops open. Mark looked around the room. Michael, Ifte, Bill, Stephanie, and Marie were there. Where was James?

"What's up?" asked Bill.

"We have a crisis. We were supposed to deliver our portion of the Pliny project last Friday. We missed the deadline. We also didn't give any warning. The project manager and the customer are livid. This was a key milestone. If we can't deliver today, there will likely be severe financial consequences to Amalgamated. I also learned from

Jeff there are other project proposals in the works from Pliny. If we fail to deliver this one, we put the others in jeopardy."

"What happened?" asked Stephanie. "According to updates during the team meeting, things were going great."

"I know," replied Mark. "This was as much of a surprise to me as it is to you."

"Where's James?" asked Ifte. "This is his project."

At that moment, James sauntered through the door.

"Where have you been?" asked Mark.

James smiled. "Taking care of things. No need to worry, I have everything under control."

"Excellent," said Mark. "So you'll have the deliverables in place before noon?"

"No. I told you this morning it will take at least a week, maybe longer."

"So how could this be resolved?" asked Mark.

"I called Diane. I told her there was no way this was going to get done today and no amount of pestering was going to help. I told her we'd have it as soon as we could. That was our job. Her job was to keep people off our backs so we could get our work done."

At that moment, Mark's cell phone started ringing. He pulled it out and glanced at the screen. It was Diane. Mark felt his stomach drop.

CHAPTER 13 – Fallout

"So what happened next?" asked Steve. It was the following day and Mark and Steve were at their regular table.

"It was awful," said Mark. His voice was muffled because he had his hands over his face. "Diane was furious. She told me if I didn't contact HR right away, she was going to. She wanted James escorted off the property. Quite frankly so did I. It seemed like he was trying to sink the project and our team.

"I promised Diane I would deal with James, but asked if I could wait until after the Pliny delivery. She reluctantly agreed."

Mark continued to explain that after his conversation with Diane, he went to James for a word in private. Once away from the rest of the team, Mark told James his actions were inappropriate, making the situation worse, and likely putting his job at risk. He explained Diane and the customer were very angry and had specifically asked that any communication regarding the Pliny project come through Mark. Finally, he stated the team had to deliver something of substance by noon, and asked where they were most likely to make progress.

At that point James erupted. He told Mark nobody at

Amalgamated was qualified to question his skills or his ability to complete work. Gesticulating wildly with fingers jabbing dangerously close to Mark's face, James said he would not stand idly by and be insulted. James ended by saying he would not offer any help or information until given an official apology from both Mark and Diane. Then, he stood and stormed out of the office, slamming the door behind him.

"I couldn't believe it," said Mark, "he had the audacity to expect me to apologize to him. Fortunately, I realized the clock was ticking and didn't try to do anything about James until later.

"Instead, I called the rest of the team to the conference room. Once they arrived, I let them know a delivery was still needed by noon, but now they needed to do it without help from James.

Mark paused. "They were speechless. It was a full minute before any of them said anything. Then Stephanie, bless her heart, said she had a copy of the design document and knew where the project work was being stored. That broke the ice and everyone started throwing out information they thought might be helpful. We quickly realized we knew almost nothing about the current status of the project. With only three hours left, they asked for an hour to do some research. With no other choice, I agreed.

"An hour later, everyone was back in the conference room. Stephanie had found the design documents, the code, and the testing plans. The team had also learned the coding was complete and testing underway. In fact, the system had passed every test case but the last. Most of the test cases were designed to see if the different components would return desired results. The last test was designed to see if the system would be able to handle large amounts of traffic. Unfortunately, as soon as the system was put under a large load, it failed.

"As we dug into the issue, Ifte noticed several of the test plans were approved by the same member of the testing team. We used the conference phone to call that tester. Before we could finish describing the situation, he stopped us. He was very familiar with the project, and remembered being yelled at and accused of incompetence. He also remembered that James refused to believe the test results even though the tester had one of his colleagues double-check everything. Before hanging up, the tester promised to send the written test results. Within 15 minutes we received the document, made copies for everyone, and were all poring over the results.

Mark paused and smiled. "Bill found the solution. As soon as he saw the error codes, he suspected the database server had been built using an old version of the software. It only took us five minutes to determine he was right. The only question left, then, was how to fix it.

"With an hour left, we called the database sales representative and explained the situation. After a tense half hour waiting for a reply, the sales representative called back and told us there were two possible solutions. The first and best option was to completely rebuild the database server, which would take between six and eight hours. The second option was to download a software patch, which would only take three hours, but might cause further problems.

Mark put his head in his hands. "The team was devastated. They had pulled together and done amazing work only to learn neither solution could be implemented within the timeline. It was heartbreaking."

"It sounds awful," said Steve. "What did you do?"

"I collected all the information and documentation, and went to tell Diane the bad news."

"When I finished delivering the news, I offered to be the

one to tell the customer. When Diane looked at me skeptically, I quickly explained that since it was my team's failure it was my responsibility to explain the situation to the customer. The team and I hoped hearing the news from those responsible would be a good first step in repairing the business relationship.

"Diane told me she wasn't sure the Pliny team would agree, but she would be glad to have me do the talking. She believed I would do a much more thorough job of explaining the situation and answering any questions."

Mark took a deep breath. "It was a long drive over to the Pliny offices. I was nervous, and I could tell Diane was too. I think we said three words to each other the entire trip. When we arrived at the reception area, we were immediately ushered to a conference room at the top of the building, and the meeting started.

"As we went around the room introducing ourselves," said Mark, "I realized Diane and I weren't the only Amalgamated staff. Sitting to the right of Pliny's CEO was Michael Peters, my CIO."

Steve shook his head. "Wow, a very tough situation."

After the introductions, Mark was on. He stood, took a deep breath and began by apologizing that they needed to meet at all. He explained the situation was due to a staffing situation he should have addressed earlier. He then outlined the current situation, describing the options his team had discovered and the advantages and risks of each. He finished by apologizing, again, and letting the group know his team was ready to implement whatever the group decided.

"How did they take the news?" asked Steve.

"Well, they weren't happy, but they thanked us for our honesty. Then they told us they'd have an answer within the hour, and excused us. As we left, Michael pulled me aside and said he wanted to meet once the situation was resolved."

Steve looked puzzled. "Did he seem angry?"

Mark shook his head. "No, not really, but he didn't look happy either. I just don't know."

Steve scratched his head. "Hmmm… We'll need to think about that later. For now, tell me how things turned out."

"Well, a half-hour later, on the dot, I got a call from the Pliny project manager. He told me they had decided to take our recommendation to do the reinstall. Even though it would take more time, they agreed the finished product would be better. I thanked them for the information and got the team working right away.

"We got everything reinstalled by seven o'clock that evening. It passed all our tests and theirs, and they were pleased with the results.

"They still decided to invoke the non-delivery clause. They told me it was because if communication had been more timely, there wouldn't have been a last minute emergency. I agreed, and took the information back to Diane and Jeff."

Steve looked Mark right in the eyes. "So how do you feel?"

Mark laughed humorlessly. "I feel terrible. The delivery was late, the team worked their backsides off to cover for James' stupid mistake, Amalgamated still had to pay the non-delivery penalty, I'm probably going to hear a thing or two when I get back to the office, and worst of all, I still have to deal with James!"

Steve shook his head. "I understand your frustration, but I see things differently. Sure there were mistakes made. Sure it wasn't pleasant. However, you and the team pulled together and came up with good options for the customer. You took responsibility for the situation and ended up delivering a great solution. The way I look at it, you and your team pulled a rabbit out of a hat. What you did was darned near miraculous."

"You think so?" Mark asked.

"I do. So stop worrying about things you can't change. Instead, let's brainstorm what to do about James."

CHAPTER 14 – Loose Ends

Two days later, Mark and Diane met with Ann from HR to file the formal complaint against James. Ann took notes as Diane recounted her story. Mark listened and asked questions to ensure he had enough information to describe James' behavior as accurately as possible.

A few hours later Mark and Ann met with Paul, Diane's supervisor. Paul had heard about the meeting with Diane and wanted to speak with them too. He had been sitting in the office when Diane received the second call from James. He told them even though he was sitting across the desk from Diane he could hear James' voice quite well. He corroborated Diane's story and even added a couple of details regarding what had been said. He finished by saying he felt the tone and content of James' communication to be threatening, and requested Mark put James under immediate disciplinary action.

Ann then asked Mark for his recollection of events. She asked if he had spoken directly with James. Mark recounted the conversation he and James had right after the initial phone call. He described James' raised voice and wild gesticulations and told her he had flinched several times because James' finger came very close to his face. He finished by telling Ann about James' refusal to work until he had received a formal apology.

As he finished Mark paused and ran his fingers through his hair. "Quite frankly, Ann, I agree with Paul. James' behavior was inappropriate and unprofessional. If he wishes to continue working on my team, his behavior needs to change. I need to tell him so. However, I have very little experience with this kind of message. I'm concerned if I say what I just told you, he'll either not take it seriously or he'll retaliate. I'd like your help."

Ann smiled reassuringly. "Don't worry Mark. Unfortunately, I have quite a bit of experience with this type of conversation. He does need to hear it from you, but I'll make certain I'm available to help. This won't be pleasant, but we'll get through it."

The two of them scheduled a meeting with James later that afternoon. Both arrived several minutes early to ensure they were prepared. Just as they finished reviewing the disciplinary action form James opened the door and strode into the room without knocking. He plopped down in the remaining chair, leaned back, and crossed his arms.

Mark sat forward and placed his forearms on the table. "James, we need to have some further discussion regarding what happened with the Pliny project."

James smiled. "Sure boss. I'm ready to get back to work as soon as you and Diane apologize."

Mark leaned across the table and placed a copy of the disciplinary action form in front of James. "That isn't why we're here." He paused and took a breath to steady himself. "I asked Ann from HR to join us because we need to talk about changes you need to make in your behavior, and I want to make certain they are communicated clearly."

James' smile disappeared. Mark picked up his notes, cleared his throat, and began to work his way through the points he and Ann had prepared. After about five minutes, James was sitting bolt upright. His eyes had narrowed and his nostrils flared. Mark also noticed that his face was completely red.

As Mark took a breath to ask if he understood, James reached out, grabbed the disciplinary action form, ripped it into several pieces, and threw them at both Mark and Ann.

"This is insulting! I refuse to work for a supervisor that has so little regard for talent and is so easily manipulated by others. You don't deserve my skills. I resign, effective immediately!" He stood and started to storm out of the room.

Ann spoke for the first time. "Just a minute James."

He turned and looked at her with contempt.

She continued in a quiet but authoritative tone. "I would encourage you to reconsider. You are skilled and can be of great value to our organization. However, your value to the organization does not excuse your behavior with Diane or the way you just treated Mark and I. We would love for you to continue working for Amalgamated, but you will need to improve the behaviors we outlined in the disciplinary action form. If you are unwilling to make those changes, resigning is your only other option.

"If you choose to resign, we will need your keys, your access badge, and your company cell phone. Furthermore, we will need you to sign a voluntary termination form or provide us with a letter of resignation that states your intent, gives an effective date, and lists an address where we can send your final paycheck.

"The choice is yours. We need your answer before the end of the day."

James looked shocked for a moment, then turned to leave the room. "You will have my keys, my badge, my phone, and my letter of resignation within the hour."

An hour later, Mark and Ann were in her office, debriefing. Without knocking he strode through the door carrying a box. He dropped the box in the chair next to Mark. Out of it he pulled a cell phone, his badge, and his keys. He tossed all of them on Ann's desk. Out of his shirt pocket he pulled a sheet of paper and dropped it in Mark's lap. Then he stood looking at both of them.

Ann folded her hands on her desktop. "It looks like you've made your decision."

James tipped his head. "I have."

Mark picked up the letter and read through it.

"To whom it may concern:

I officially resign my position at Amalgamated, effective immediately. Any final paperwork and pay I am owed may be sent to the address given at the top of this letter.

Sincerely,

James Mehta."

"It looks in order to me," said Mark as he passed it to Ann.

She glanced at it and nodded. "I agree."

Mark stood up and turned to James, holding out his hand. "I am sorry you've made this decision, but I wish you well."

James ignored Mark's hand. He nodded once, then picked up his box and left the room.

When the door had closed behind him, Ann looked at Mark. "We need to have his computer accesses terminated immediately."

Mark took a deep breath and rose to leave. "I'll go make it happen."

Ann stopped him. "Mark, don't take this too hard. He made his own decisions. And, quite frankly, I think it will work out best for both he and your team. You did really well during a very difficult situation."

He stopped with his hand on the door. "Thanks." He turned to look at her. "You know, I agree with you but I sure don't feel good about it."

Ann smiled. "That's part of what makes you a good supervisor."

CHAPTER 15 – The Rest Of Maribelle's Story

As soon as Mark got back to his office, he dialed Steve's number.

"This is Steve," he heard after three rings.

"Hey Steve, this is Mark. I'm not having a good day and was wondering if you might have time to talk today or tomorrow? I feel the quicksand pulling me down, and I need some help swimming."

"Let's see. I have a meeting at 1 this afternoon, but could be available at 4. Would that work?"

"That would be great. I'll see you then." Mark hung up.

For the next couple of hours he tried to be productive but his mind kept drifting. He either found himself replaying the meeting with James or worrying about why the CIO wanted to meet. After dragging himself back on task several times he gave up, shut down his computer, and headed out of the office.

His car clock read 3:30 when he pulled into Maribelle's parking lot. When he walked in the door, Maribelle met him with her customary smile. When he didn't smile back her smile fell.

"What's the matter? You look like you just lost your best friend."

Mark recounted his morning to her. As he spoke, she nodded.

"It sounds like you had one hell of a day. He must have been really upset to resign like that. Still, it sounds like you did the right thing. He had no right to treat the project manager that way. As his supervisor, you had to bring that to his attention. I know it probably doesn't help much, but I'm sure things will end up working out. Stop being so hard on yourself."

Mark looked at her. "What makes you so sure things will work out?"

"Because I used to be James."

Mark's jaw dropped. "You? No way!"

"Yes Mark, I was. I didn't tell my supervisor or project manager to back off. Nor did I blatantly put a project in jeopardy the way it sounds like he did. However, I did become a liability to the company and my work unit."

Maribelle took a moment to remind Mark of the situation in which she found herself at her old job, then began to tell the rest of her story. "The truth is, even though Steve and I kept working to improve my standing within the company, I was crushed by what my supervisor and the division manager put me through. I began to see little things about the company that should be corrected and started speaking up about them. At first, I truly meant to help, but as time went on I became more and more cynical.

"It's embarrassing to look back. I became a master of the sweetly sarcastic statement. I could kill an idea or derail a conversation with a look and a couple of comments. I began to revel in the power I had, paying little attention to who I hurt. Finally, my manager had enough. He called me into his office and outlined the changes I needed to make if I was to stay on the team.

"You know what the worst part was?" she asked Mark.

Mark shook his head.

"He was right. In the beginning, I had reasons to be upset with him, but I had lost my moral high ground. I had, essentially, stooped to his level. I was angry at myself."

"What did you do?" Mark asked.

"I resigned."

"Why?"

She thought for a moment. "Well, I realized my supervisor and I were never going to get along. And, because of how connected he was, I was going to have to work around him in order to be successful. When he outlined the changes I'd need to make I realized he was right, and I had two options--change or leave. When I thought about changing, I felt tired rather than excited. I was afraid that no matter what I did, my supervisor and I would be at odds at some point and all my work would have been for nothing. Resigning was hard but it felt right--right for me and right for the company."

"What happened then?"

"I refocused my work with Steve and the most amazing thing happened. I discovered my passion."

Mark raised his eyebrows.

Maribelle smiled. "I'd always enjoyed cooking and regularly brought food with me when I met with Steve. He would listen politely while I described how I'd made each dish, then rave about how good it tasted. After about the millionth compliment, he asked if I'd ever considered opening a restaurant. I told him I hadn't because I knew it was a tough business--the margins are low and the hours terrible. He just smiled and nodded and we moved on to other topics. But, the seed was planted. The idea of running a restaurant felt right, but I couldn't ignore how hard I thought it would be to be successful. Finally, I sat down and actually ran numbers with a friend of mine who was an accountant for several successful restaurants. He told me where he thought the sweet spots were for prices, expenses, etc. Then, he introduced me to a couple of his out of town clients who were more than happy to share information. The more I learned, the more excited I became.

"At my next meeting with Steve, I officially changed our focus. Within a month, we put together the basic plan for what you see today."

From behind him he heard Steve say, "Not we, Maribelle, you. I just asked questions and helped you stay focused. All the work and all the passion were yours. That's why you've been so successful."

Mark hadn't heard him come through the door and he jumped at the sound of Steve's voice.

Maribelle just smiled. "And the rest, as they say, is history. That's why I know things will get better. They did for me. Right before I resigned I was mad at my boss for being such a jerk; I was mad at leadership for enabling him and not supporting me; and I was mad at the company for letting me down. After I resigned I was mad because nothing bad happened to them. Secretly, I wished I'd get a phone call saying they needed me back. It never happened.

"I didn't see it right away, but now it's obvious I never would have been happy if I'd stayed. I'm sure your former employee will find the same to be true."

Mark smiled. "Thanks for sharing that. It helps."

"No problem," said Maribelle. Then she turned him to face their table and gently nudged both of them toward it. "Now you two go talk about what to do next."

CHAPTER 16 – The Surprise

The meeting with Steve and Maribelle allowed Mark to calm down at least a little. Maribelle's story helped Mark feel better about the outcome of the situation between he, Diane and James. The brainstorming with Steve helped him feel better about options going forward.

During the weekend, Mark, Maggie and Denise visited one of the local beaches for an afternoon. For the most part, he was able to put the week behind him and focus on enjoying time with the two of them. There was only once when Maggie caught him staring off into space with a frown on his face. She poked him playfully in the ribs and reminded him there would be plenty of time for work during the week.

She'd been right. The weekend had flown by. In no time at all it was 8 o'clock Monday morning and his to-do list was already too long for one day. "Well," he thought to himself, "at least I don't have to worry about losing my job because there isn't enough work."

He finished up some edits on a project report and was getting ready to hit send when his phone rang.

He picked it up. "IT. This is Mark."

"Hello Mark. This is Kimberly, Michael Peters' Administrative Assistant."

"Crud," thought Mark. It had been over a week, and he'd been hoping the CIO had forgotten about meeting with him.

Mark took a deep breath. "Hello Kimberly, what can I do for you?"

"Michael was wondering if you'd be available to meet this morning. I looked at calendars and noticed you were both free at ten. Because it's such short notice, I thought I'd call rather than just sending the invitation. Does ten work for you?"

"Ten would be great. Are we meeting in Michael's office?"

"If that's okay with you," Kimberly replied. "Michael has several meetings afterward and it would help him stay on schedule."

"That works fine for me. I'll be there. Thanks for the call."

"I'll see you in about an hour. Thank you for your flexibility, Mark."

As Mark hung up the phone, his hands started to sweat. Here goes nothing, he thought to himself.

****

Mark arrived at Kimberly's desk with two minutes to spare. Kimberly looked at her phone and told Mark that Michael was still on his 9 o'clock teleconference. She offered a chair and said she'd let him know when Michael was ready.

As he sat down, he began thinking about the last few months and how much had changed. When he first started working with Steve, he was ready to chuck his career at Amalgamated out the window. He felt overworked, underappreciated, and burned out.

Now things were quite different. He was seeing improvements just about everywhere. During one-on-one meetings each team member had mentioned how enjoyable work had become. Their productivity had increased, too.

In the last two months they started and completed 15% more projects than normal. They made major upgrades to three of their most critical systems. To cap things off none of the systems they were supporting had experienced any major outages or significant issues.

Successfully completing that much work with so little budgetary impact was unheard of at Amalgamated. Most surprising was that all of this occurred without increasing staffing or a significant increase in time at work. Mark smiled and shrugged to himself. It just seemed his team was happier and therefore, working more efficiently.

Even though the improvements within the team were important, he realized the most significant changes were within him. He now cared about the work and found it interesting. He realized how much he cared about his team members and wanted them to succeed. In fact, during the past week he had put together several ideas to give members of the team more visibility and responsibility. He was excited to discuss them.

Suddenly it hit him. He didn't care as much about a new title as he did about the success of his team. As long as he focused on that, things would go well. He smiled to himself, wondering how long Steve had been trying to get him to realize it.

Kimberly interrupted his thoughts. "Mark, he's finished. You can go in now."

"Thank you," he said as he stood up.

Michael appeared at his door. When he saw Mark he smiled. "Come on in, I am glad you could be available on such short notice." He pointed to a seat by his desk and closed the door behind them.

CHAPTER 17 – One Year Later

Mark and Maggie walked into Maribelle's. The restaurant was bustling with activity. As they sidled up to the host station, Maribelle winked and waved.

Mark smiled and nodded, then leaned over and whispered to Maggie so that Maribelle could hear. "I'm glad we called and made a reservation. The place is packed."

Maribelle smiled, leaned in and whispered back. "If you hadn't called, I'd have made you sweat, but we'd have found someplace to seat you."

Maggie laughed. "And we really appreciate it. This is, by far, our favorite restaurant."

Maribelle smiled from ear to ear. "I'm very glad to hear that."

"It looks like it's everyone else's too," said Mark.

Maribelle looked around at the full tables. "It does, doesn't it?" Then she looked at the list in front of her. "Your table is ready to go. In fact, it looks like your dinner partners snuck past me. My list says they're already here."

"Excellent," said Mark. "Our normal table?"

"Of course! Where else would we seat you?" said Maribelle with feigned hurt. "May I show you to your place?"

Swimming In Quicksand

"Absolutely!" said Mark and Maggie at the same time.

Maribelle grabbed two menus and led them to the same table Mark and Steve had shared many times over the past 18 months.

As they reached the table, Steve stood and held out his hand. "Mark, it's great to see you." Then he turned to Maggie. "And Maggie, you look stunning this evening."

Maggie smiled and blushed. Then she leaned down and greeted Bethany, Steve's wife. "It's great to see you. How are the boys?"

The four of them spent a few minutes catching up and deciding what to order for dinner. As they waited for their drinks, talk turned to how things were going with their work.

After Steve gave an overview of how his practice was going, he asked Mark how he was enjoying his new job at Amalgamated. Mark paused before answering. It had been a whirlwind year, all beginning when he met with his CIO. During that meeting he was sure they would be discussing steps Amalgamated might take to ensure similar situations never happened again. However, Michael surprised him completely.

Michael started the conversation by congratulating Mark on how well he had handled himself during a very stressful situation. He was specifically impressed by how Mark had taken complete responsibility for the situation, apologized, then rather than dwelling on what had gone wrong, offered options for how the situation could be corrected.

Then, Michael mentioned he had recently reviewed the performance of Mark's team and had been impressed by their numbers. It was obvious the team was highly motivated and focused on success. Michael asked several questions about which strategies were successful and which weren't.

Mark was beginning to really enjoy the conversation

when Michael leaned back in his chair and said he needed to come to the point of the meeting.

Mark felt his chest tighten. He had entered the meeting thinking Michael wanted to discuss his poor performance on the Pliny project. While Michael had given him several compliments, he was sure the other shoe was about to drop.

"Mark," Michael started. "I'm not sure how to say this, so I'm just going to come out with it..." He ran his fingers through his hair, then straightened up and continued. "We have several projects that aren't going as planned. Many of them are for customers we'd like to make long-term partners. I'm putting together a new division that works specifically with high potential customers. Based on your performance, I would like for you to consider managing one of the units within that organization. Would you be interested?"

Mark was speechless. Had he heard correctly? "I'm sorry Michael, did you just offer me a different job?"

Michael smiled and nodded. Not only was he offering Mark a different job, but a promotion and a healthy raise, too.

After the initial shock wore off, Mark was able to learn that Michael believed this division would be one of the keys to keeping the company afloat in the uncertain economy. If Mark accepted, Michael wanted him to meet with the rest of the division's leadership to develop a staffing proposal that would allow them to be successful without being too big. Michael wanted agility and quick results.

The transition went quickly. Within a week, Mark had spoken with his current supervisor and Maggie, and gotten their approval and support. Maggie was ecstatic, and he learned Jeff would be moving to the new division too. Two days later, he accepted the position. Within a month he met the rest of the divisional leadership, wrote his staffing proposal, and received approval to move it forward. Three weeks after that, he hired all of his previous team and four new individuals.

Soon after everyone was hired, they received their first assignment. A local Fortune 1000 company had recently fired another IT firm for missing three deadlines. They were trying to launch a new service and had contracts and customer service level agreements on the line. They needed an immediate solution.

Mark and his team used the five 'O's to put their plans together. While he wasn't certain if it would work, he figured with a little tweaking, the formal approach would help them make certain they explored the situation thoroughly. The team found that creating an overview and objectives helped focus their thinking. Brainstorming options, then looking for obstacles, helped them create multiple solutions. Creating an operational plan before starting the actual work meant fewer issues arose during execution. Thinking through these steps usually didn't take them long. In fact, it seemed to save them time in the long run.

Mark also decided to change his approach to leadership. In the past, he had assumed a command and control stance by doing the initial assessment and planning himself, assigning resulting tasks to the team, then monitoring results. His work with Steve had demonstrated the individuals on the team had many underutilized talents and they were capable of much more than he had allowed. This time, Mark decided to bring the team the raw requirements and try coaching them through the entire project.

After some pointers from Steve and a few planning sessions, the team was able to dig in and create a platform that wasn't perfect, but allowed the customer to meet all their obligations. Plus, they delivered it three days ahead of the deadline. Three weeks later, they followed up with an upgrade that corrected a couple of minor issues and enhancements that surpassed the customer's initial expectations.

Over the next several months, Mark's team was able to create similar results for other customers too. The rest of the division was also doing very well, but Mark's unit became known as the SWAT Team--the group to send in when the chips were down and the stakes high. The net result for Amalgamated was over six million dollars in new business. This was double the company growth from the past year. Michael was pleased with the division's track record and specifically impressed with the success of Mark's team.

Even as things improved, Mark and Steve continued to work together. While Mark was happy with his progress, he wanted to make certain he had a well-defined plan to help guide his future career choices. In the past he had left things to chance and firmly believed this was how he ended up stuck. His experience with Steve taught him how much control he could have if he knew what he wanted and had a plan to get there.

The career planning ended up paying off. Just a month ago, Michael had approached him with a new leadership opportunity. While the offer sounded attractive, it ran counter to several of the career guidelines and goals he and Steve had documented. The new position offered a larger salary, but meant spending more time away from his family and leaving the team he had just built.

Mark was torn. Would he be limiting future growth opportunities by declining this position? He stewed on it for a while, but finally decided to talk with Michael about his concerns.

It was the right decision. When Mark mentioned he didn't feel comfortable accepting the position because it didn't align with his current or long-term goals, Michael was disappointed but impressed. He shook his head and smiled, noting that career planning would be much easier if everyone spent the same amount of effort to discover what they wanted. He was eager to learn more about Mark's plans.

The two of them spent considerable time discussing Mark's desires and goals. They ended by agreeing Mark would continue to lead the SWAT efforts for now and Michael would keep his eyes open for opportunities that aligned with Mark's goals.

Mark smiled to himself. It had been a very good year indeed. He finally felt like he had stopped thrashing. He no longer felt like his job was pulling him under. He was actually swimming. He smiled again. He was "swimming in quicksand."

"So, do you feel like you accomplished your goals?" asked Steve.

Mark beamed. "Definitely."

"Excellent. What will you do next?"

"I'd like to pay things forward," answered Mark.

"What do you mean?"

"Well, if you have some time, I have a couple of people I've been helping with their career plans. They could use your expertise."

Steve shrugged. "Now that you and I aren't meeting as often, I should have some time. What are they struggling with?"

"Well, they've got a lot of really good ideas, and they're very excited. However, they keep struggling to create actionable plans, and as you've told me on more than one occasion..."

Steve, Mark, Maggie, and Betsy all chimed in together. "A plan without action isn't worth squat!"

They all laughed, then Steve raised his glass. "To the Five

O's!"
    Mark raised his. "To swimming in quicksand!"
    Maggie raised hers. "To sanity!"
    They all laughed again and clinked glasses. "To sanity!"

CHAPTER 18 – Coaching Overview

While Mark's story is fictional, and not everyone's situation will end as happily, many do. In my experience, those that have a plan and work diligently toward their objectives often succeed.

Unfortunately there are a significant number of people who don't have a plan. According to a Gallup survey, fewer than half of US workers (41%) started their career through conscious choice. At a recent meeting I attended, an informal poll showed that fewer than 25% had a defined career plan. Another source noted that up to 32% of employees don't know their next move within their organization.

To be fair, even without career planning some people do fine. Unfortunately, most fall into one of two categories. They either watch peers progress while they don't, or they regularly climb the career ladder, but never identify what opportunities will make them happy. For the first group, it is obvious why they might be unhappy. For the second, they continually cycle between excitement and boredom. They may achieve high levels of positional and income success, but often feel something is missing. Even though the results seem different, both groups are stuck.

The bottom line: Without a specific, focused career plan you are playing the career lottery. Like the real lottery, the likelihood you will happen upon a position you find exciting and fulfilling is relatively slim. However, if you take time to decide what you want and make reasoned, focused steps in that direction, your success is almost guaranteed. With that in mind, following the same steps Mark and Steve took should not only put you on a path toward a more satisfying career, but will significantly increase your odds of being successful.

So, where should you start?

Mark's first step was to take responsibility for his situation and change his attitude and approach to work. This change of attitude is one of the most difficult steps to take, yet one of the most important. Many people, including me, find it hard to admit they may be limiting their own opportunities. Rather than looking for ways to improve themselves, they spend a tremendous amount of effort looking outward for explanations—office politics, crappy managers, unfair policies, favoritism, etc.

While all these exist, they usually aren't the real problem. Most people remain stuck because they continue to work the same way they always have, yet expect others to view them differently. In contrast, most successful people are willing to take feedback and able to make changes.

Even if you are stuck due to one of the external issues listed above, you aren't powerless. By not giving up, looking inward, and working on yourself rather than becoming a victim, you will likely find multiple ways out of your current situation. They just might not be within your current organization.

Another important step for Mark was to create a plan. While nobody can control everything, success is much more likely if you are actively working toward a specific goal. To help ensure your success, your plan should be reasonably detailed, practical, realistic, and action oriented. As Steve noted, "Without action, plans don't mean squat."

It can be hard to come up with a plan that meets all these criteria. That's where tools can be helpful. While Steve and Mark used the five O's to organize their work, there are many tools available. GROW, GOOD, OSCAR, SUCCESS, and the five steps of Appreciative Inquiry are just a few. Each can be effective. Each has strengths and weaknesses. Some coaches will use just one, while others use multiple tools. It all depends upon the situation. The bottom line is to use something that moves you toward the results you want.

Let's take a closer look at the tool Steve and Mark used.

The five O's

A few words of introduction might be in order before diving into the specifics of the five O's. While Mark and Steve worked through each O successively, not everyone will. As with most coaching tools, consider each O as part of a checklist. For example, if you already have a strong idea of where you want to go or what you want to change, it may make sense to start with objectives. However, if you are struggling to decide what to change it may make more sense to start with an overview. Additionally, professional coaches may suggest starting with some sort of overview because it is a good way for the two of you to familiarize yourselves with each other.

Now, let's review each O.

Overview

To create a successful plan, you need to know two things: Where you are now and where you'd like to be. The overview is a way to help you explore and understand your current situation. What are your strengths and weaknesses? What knowledge and skills do you possess? What opportunities exist and what obstacles might get in your way? Think of this as your personal SWOT (strengths, weaknesses, opportunities, and threats) exercise.

When looking at your current situation, look for as many sources of information as you can. These might include:
- ✓ Talking to your supervisor.
- ✓ Reviewing current and past performance appraisals.
- ✓ Asking friends and family what they believe your strengths and weaknesses are.
- ✓ Talking to co-workers.
- ✓ Talking to partners (if you are self-employed)
- ✓ Talking to people who come to you for service of some kind.
- ✓ Talking to your mentor (if you have one).
- ✓ Investigating past successes and failures to look for trends.
- ✓ Taking inventories or tests such as the MBTI, EQI, or Strengths-Finder (TM).
- ✓ Asking someone to follow you around and observe your performance or behavior.

While there might not be time to do all of these things, and some of them might not be appropriate for your situation, anything that can provide constructive feedback should be considered. The more information you can collect, the clearer the picture.

A word of caution is necessary here. It can be very easy to go from being coached to being counseled. There are several issues, both ethical and legal, that arise when the line between coaching and counseling is crossed. So how can you tell the difference? Probably the easiest is to remember that coaching should be focused on the future. For both coaching and counseling, it is important to understand your current situation--your skills, knowledge, strengths, and weaknesses. However, coaching is not about delving into or dwelling on the past. If you find situations where you feel you need to dig into your past in order to feel better about your future, you should seek out a licensed counseling professional. If you are working with a good coach, they will be able to recognize the difference and point you in the right direction.

Objectives

If the overview is used to determine where you are, defining objectives is how you determine where you want to be. While you probably started the change process with some kind of goal, this exercise is about creating measurable, time-bound specifics.

To be measurable your objective needs to include some way to identify when you are done. What will you or others see or experience once you have reached your objective? What will be different? Is there something you will be able to hand someone, like a certificate? Is there a new service you will be delivering? Will there be a change to a metric or performance criteria?

Time-bound means to set a deadline—the more specific the better. "This year", is too broad. "Next quarter" is too. August 15th, 2015 might be too far away, but it is very specific. "Before our meeting next week" is also a good example of a specific deadline.

Finally, once you have your objectives identified, it is very important to put them in writing. This accomplishes two things. Most obviously, it provides evidence of your commitment. Writing also helps you think through the process and provide clarification. I have seen more than one occasion where writing down objectives provided key insights that ensured success.

Options

Once you have objectives set, it's time to brainstorm how to achieve them. During this step consider everything you think will help achieve your objectives. What classes are available? What individuals have valuable information or experience? What opportunities, projects or assignments will provide needed experience? What books should you read? What seminars should you attend? What offices should you hold? Write down everything that occurs to you. Everything. At this point, every idea is a good idea. Your goal should be to have the largest list you can create.

Operations

Here is where the "rubber meets the road". After you've created as large a list of options as you can, you will need to narrow that list down to the few things you will work to accomplish. However, as Steve noted, this needs to be more than just a list of actions. To make actions operational, you must decide what needs to be done, what order, by when, and how you will know the action is complete.

Perhaps the most important part of this step is to identify someone to hold you accountable. If you are working with a professional coach, that need has been met. A good coach will definitely hold you accountable. However, if you are working alone, I highly recommend seeking out an individual or individuals you trust and asking them to help.

Please don't skip identifying someone to hold you accountable. For most people, it is easy to justify missing a goal or not fulfilling a self-appointed obligation. Engaging someone to hold you accountable makes your commitment public. Once you've shared your plans with someone else and asked them to help, you are much more likely to follow-through.

Obstacles

This is another critical step that is too often skipped. I have seen many individuals create great plans only to give up at the first sign of adversity. My hypothesis is they gave up because the difficulty surprised them. Don't be surprised. If the change is worthwhile, things are likely to get difficult. If what you want to do were easy you would have already accomplished it.

The purpose of this 'O' is to ensure that when trouble arises you have some sort of plan. This means it is imperative to both identify obstacles and prepare responses for them.

What kind of response? Well, the best response would be one that avoids the obstacle all together. However, for some you will need to create mitigation strategies. It might mean building a helpful relationship. It might mean creating a work-around or alternative. It could mean just acknowledging the obstacle occurred, putting your head down, and working through it. In any case, the point is to be prepared for set-backs and keep moving forward.

For example, one of Mark's objectives was to have his team attend more of the meetings. In reality, if he had just added the meetings to their calendars, they would likely have pushed back. However, since he and Steve had thought through what their reaction might be, he was able to make the connection about providing them opportunities for growth. By already having made that connection he was not only more prepared for the conversation, but likely more confident, too.

It is probably worth adding a word of caution here. It

will be impossible to consider every obstacle. Trying to do so could lead to "analysis paralysis." If you are able to identify the most likely obstacles and create plans for them, often those plans will also cover other obstacles you might not have identified.

After you have considered all five O's, you should have a fairly robust plan. Now comes the really hard part—taking action. This is where many fail. If you've come this far and are struggling, here are some pointers that can help.

First, write your plans down. As noted previously, writing can help clarify thoughts and actions. The act of writing goals and plans has also been linked by several studies to an increased likelihood of success.

Second, make your plans public. Get family and friends involved. Announce them at a gathering, post them on a website, or write about them using your favorite social networking tool. Ask friends and acquaintances to remind you of your plans and help you stick to them.

Finally, I would recommend hiring a professional coach. While your friends and family can be effective, it can sometimes be difficult for them to deliver tough messages, point out blind-spots, or hold you accountable for fulfilling commitments. Further, coaches have tools and experience your friends and family may not.

Finally, once you've started making progress, don't stop. As Steve told Mark once they had the initial planning out of the way, "do, review, rinse, and repeat." Improvement and growth are cyclic processes. Begin by making changes you are pretty certain will succeed. Review the outcomes and see how things are working out. Then, use the results to plan for future steps.

Don't be afraid to change your plan if necessary. Be

flexible. Keep doing, reviewing, rinsing, and repeating until you reach the outcome you want. Then look for your next outcome.

Whether you are self-employed or a corporate employee, the only way to guarantee success is by creating a plan and working through it.

Yes, I said guarantee.

If you put together your plan and stick with it you will grow, and you will get un-stuck. I promise. So, what are you waiting for?

ABOUT THE AUTHOR

Scott Koon holds a Master of Arts in Management and a Bachelor's Degree in Music and Computer Science. He has over 21 years experience in the Information Technology industry and 16 years of management experience. He facilitates Crucial Conversations® and Emotional Intelligence classes, helps individuals with career planning, and has spoken regularly at regional, national, and international conferences. Most recently he developed and facilitates a formal mentoring program at a large health care organization in the upper Midwest. He loves to fly airplanes and lives with his wife, daughter and their cat in Minnesota.

www.ingramcontent.com/pod-product-compliance
Lightning Source LLC
Chambersburg PA
CBHW051728170526
45167CB00002B/846